by Jim Denison, PhD
and Ryan Denison, MDiv

HOW DOES GOD SEE AMERICA?

DENISON FORUM®
NEWS DISCERNED DIFFERENTLY

How Does God See America?

TABLE OF CONTENTS

PREFACE

It is a rare privilege for an author to write a book with his son. Such has been my honor with the book you are now reading.

Ryan Denison completed a bachelor of arts in religion at Baylor University and earned a master of divinity degree at Truett Seminary. He is now completing his dissertation for his doctorate in church history at B. H. Carroll Theological Institute. For several years, Ryan has worked with me in research and writing. He writes *The Daily Article* when I am on vacation and has contributed many articles to our website.

This is our first book together. Ryan wrote the introduction and the conclusion. He organized and edited the rest of the book, supplying essential content and context. *How Does God See America?* would not exist without his outstanding partnership.

In addition, I want to express my gratitude to Blake Atwood for his masterful copyediting. I also want to thank Chris Elkins, Melissa Tjarks, and Drake Holtry for their essential contributions to the creation, publication, and marketing of the project. I want to thank the entire Denison Ministries team for the privilege of serving God with you each day.

And Ryan and I want to thank our wives and families for your wonderful and consistent support. You make our lives and work a great joy.

PREFACE

This is my eleventh book. Never before have I worked with so talented a team of partners. To God be the glory.

Jim Denison
March 2019,
Dallas, Texas

Notes: Unless otherwise noted, all biblical citations are from the New International Version, 2011 edition. Also, our ministry published a booklet three years ago titled *How Does God See America?* This book greatly expands the thesis of that earlier work.

INTRODUCTION:
IS THE END NEAR? OR DOES
AMERICA STILL HAVE TIME?

How does God see America? Are we that "city on a hill" that the Pilgrims and others across our nation's history set out to be? Or are we more akin to a fallen and corrupt Israel standing on the precipice of divine judgment?

In a nation as diverse and divided as our own, is it even possible to speak of America as having a sufficiently singular identity for the question to be valid?

These are not easy questions to answer, but their difficulty in no way lessens their importance. Ours is a nation in desperate need of a word from the Lord, and that's not likely to come from political pundits or social media. If we truly want to understand what God thinks of our country, the only source we can reliably trust is his word. And while God obviously never spoke of the United States in the Bible, the principles he set down in its pages are timeless and relevant to every culture.

What pleased or grieved him four millennia ago still pleases or grieves him today.

Speaking through the prophets

Outside the teachings of Jesus Christ, the most direct word that the Lord gave to his people (and to us by extension) came through the prophets. From the time of Moses through the close of the Old Testament, God's people chose to interact with him through those who took on the mantle of prophet (cf. Exodus 20:18–19). The records we have of his interactions with those select few individuals across Israel's history function as the clearest window into his heart and mind.

If we want to know the Lord's heart for our country, the best place to start is by looking at the records of his heart for Israel. That is not to say that America is the new Israel or a people chosen by God in the same way as were the twelve tribes of Jacob.

Scripture is clear, however, that God sent his word to all peoples through the prophets and that his definitions of sin and righteousness did not vary with nationality. While his relationship with Israel was unique, he held pagans just as accountable for their actions as he did the Jews.[1] Consequently, the lessons he gave ancient peoples regarding his definitions of sin and righteousness apply to us today as well.

So, what were some of the chief points of emphasis between God and the various nations during biblical times? His relationship with them centered on three basic questions:

1. Did they respect his truth?

2. Did they respect each other?

3. Did they respect him?

To be sure, such an assessment is necessarily simplistic, but it offers us a solid framework on which to examine our country today. Subsequent sections will take a more in-depth look at each of these questions, revealing areas in which we are doing well and those that call for drastic changes.

Awakenings that changed America

When the Pilgrims first sought refuge in the New World to practice their faith in accordance with their interpretation of Scripture, they firmly believed that God would use their presence to help change the world. They saw themselves as the city on a hill that Jesus described in Matthew 5:14 and established their culture with the firm expectation that it would help prepare the way for the second coming of the Lord.

Tragically, it only took a few generations for their efforts to devolve into the same kind of religious oppression that they had sought to escape in England. This pharisaical religiosity increasingly drove younger generations from the faith and demonstrates how difficult it can be to continually follow God.

The First Great Awakening, however, shows how quickly we can turn back to the Lord. It helped to reestablish a genuine hunger for God throughout the colonies. In so doing, this transformative movement laid much of the foundation for the American Revolution and a government firmly established on Judeo-Christian morality.

Unfortunately, even the lessons of great men like Jonathan Edwards, George Whitfield, and John Wesley were not enough to keep Americans from quickly forgetting their allegiance to the Lord. Less than a decade after we won our freedom from Great Britain, George Washington lamented the degraded state of American society, remarking that "virtue, I fear, has, in a great degree, taken its departure from our land." [2]

However, God was not done with this nation just because this nation seemed increasingly to be done with God. The prayers of the faithful remnant led to the dawn of the Second Great Awakening and the revivals that helped bring the gospel to life once again for people throughout the country.

For the first half of the 1800s and through various programs and churches established thereafter, America once again appeared to be headed on a trajectory that God could bless. [3] The thirst for biblically based instruction had seldom been higher. Americans cared for each other: abolitionist movements found their origins in the revival cultures of the North while missions both at home and abroad proliferated throughout the land. And they cared about God, starting an abundance of diverse churches to bring communities of people into his presence regularly.

As is typically the case, however, the impact of the Great Awakenings would again fade. We have yet to see a revival of their scale in the century and a half since. At least, that is the case in this nation.

Similar revivals have swept through other regions of the world, but the West has largely remained unaffected. Why? There seems little doubt that the Father yearns to save souls here in the same way that he does people of other nations, but, ultimately, as Philip Yancey noted, God goes where he's wanted. [4] For many of the reasons we will discuss in this book, America seems largely separated from the work of the Lord going on elsewhere.

It would be a mistake, however, to assume that our country is beyond his reach.

Is America exceptional?

Even though the United States may have lost its desire to be God's city on a hill, we have largely retained that longing to have other nations look to us as an example. For better or worse, American exceptionalism is alive and well, as evidenced by the multitude of ways that we retain and fiercely defend our influence around the globe.

Perhaps there was always an element of pride in the desire to be that city on a hill, but, apart from the larger mission of establishing God's kingdom, that hubris has only increased in motivating Americans to dominate the world stage.

However, lest we judge our leaders too harshly, it's entirely understandable that when we can't find our inspiration from God, we would seek it from ourselves. If we don't have God as our standard, where else would we look except to each other?

When we have tried to reshape other nations in our image, some have been helped but others have not. This fact, however, is a critique only in so far as we recognize that there was a better alternative.

Absent the drive to be a city on a hill to expand God's kingdom, we're not convinced that such an alternative exists. Here we see both the capacity for good left within all people and the inherent limitations of living apart from a personal relationship with our creator.

In short, if the nearly four hundred years since the Pilgrims first landed have taught us anything, it should be that we are a people capable of doing much good but that we will never be great without God.

A quick look at our present situation only further demonstrates this basic truth.

How should we judge America?

If you polled Americans, asking to what degree they thought our nation was heading in a good direction, you would likely receive a variety of answers. This is because there are many definitions of a "good direction," but even more because there is so much evidence for both good and bad in America.

The question is therefore not, "Is America good?" but "*Where* is America good?" Conversely, the question is not, "Are American culture and morality lacking?" but "*Where* are they lacking?"

An even more urgent question: In which direction is the scale leaning? While Scripture is clear that no society will ever be entirely without sin this side of heaven, God's word also leaves little doubt that a culture can reach a point at which he deems it necessary to intervene, typically in the form of discipline.

Such an observation brings us back, however, to one of our initial questions: Can America be viewed as having a sufficiently singular identity to warrant national judgment? Our government is by no means the kind of theocracy or monarchy that ruled Israel throughout the Old Testament. And while each of us can play a role in electing our leaders, we would seldom say that they speak for us at all times. Consequently, can the same standards apply?

This question will be examined at greater length in subsequent chapters, but, for now, it is worth noting that when God sent word through the prophets to condemn Israel, it was not just because the Israelites were being led by an evil king, but rather because the people, in general, had embraced his evil ways as well.

If the Lord is going to bring judgment on America, it will be for the same reason.

In this book, we will examine issues within our culture about which God cares most. We will look at these issues through the lens of Scripture, seeking to know not only what our Lord thinks about them but also what his people can do about them.

Unless and until judgment falls on us, it is important to remember that we serve a Lord who takes no pleasure in punishment. Rather, as the prophet Joel reminded his people, God "is gracious and compassionate, slow to anger and abounding in love" (Joel 2:13). It is vital that we learn to see our culture without becoming discouraged by the bad or lulled into complacency by the good.

This balance can be difficult to maintain, but it is the only way to remain objective and work for the moral and spiritual awakening we need.

How does God judge nations?

If our goal is an objective, biblically based understanding of where our culture stands before God, it is necessary to first spend some time examining how God assesses a culture. As noted previously, three main categories appear throughout the prophets and seem to be the criterion on which God evaluates a nation:

1. Do they respect his truth?

2. Do they respect each other?

3. Do they respect him?

The question of how God evaluates a culture's respect for his truth can be difficult since different cultures have different levels of exposure to his commands. In biblical times, for example, Israel was held to a different standard than the other nations. This was because they received a direct word from the Lord through his Law and the prophets. And they were charged with living in such a way that they could communicate God's word to other nations as well (Genesis 12:2–3).[5] While other nations were still held accountable for how they disobeyed God's laws, typically such discipline was for the sort of violence and abominable actions that should not have required direct instruction to avoid.[6]

What is more pertinent to the question of a nation's respect for God's truth, however, is how they responded when it was given. In this regard, the foreign nations, at times, exceeded Israel in repentance.

God's word through the prophet Jeremiah reveals the Lord's exasperation with his people after they not only rejected his prophets but continued to neglect his word or demonstrate genuine remorse even when his judgment began (Jeremiah 2:30; 3:10). By comparison, when the people of Nineveh were presented with a portent of judgment from Jonah, "A fast was proclaimed, and all of them, from the greatest to the least, put on sackcloth" (Jonah 3:5). As a result, they were spared when Israel was not.

While not every nation responded as the Ninevites did, their example demonstrates the degree to which the Lord values those who not only believe his truth but also act upon it. That no people group is exempted from this requirement is perhaps best demonstrated by the fact that, within a generation, God would use the people who repented to conquer Israel and judge those who remained unrepentant.[7]

It would be a grave mistake for us to conclude that God cares any less about how a nation responds to his truth today than he did then. The same is true for how we choose to treat each other. While much of the discipline inflicted on biblical nations was a result of their disregard for his laws, that disregard often took the form of abusing other people. Violence against foreigners (Amos 1:3), the helpless (Amos 2:6–7), and the unborn (Amos 1:13) were all cited as reasons for God's judgment.

And while warfare was a normal part of life in biblical times, God stepped in when people began to delight in cruelty toward others and saw those around them as fundamentally lesser than themselves. In short, when people forgot that each human life was inherently valuable, the Lord took steps to remind them of just how wrong they were.

That lack of respect for each other, in turn, demonstrates a lack of respect for God. The quickest way to prove how little you care for a parent is to treat his or her children poorly. At the same time, people in the era of the prophets showed their lack of interest in the Father in other ways as well. Rampant idolatry characterized the Hebrew people throughout this period, infiltrating their borders because of the nations that surrounded them.

Such idolatry eroded the relationship between God and his children for a number of reasons. In many cases, the worship of false gods included behavior that ranged from disgraceful to abominable. The worship of Yahweh as only one God among many demonstrated a fundamentally flawed understanding of his nature, damaging their relationship with him.

Most of the Israelites who worshiped Baal or other pagan deities did so in addition to their worship of the one true God. They believed the Lord was content to be seen as one among many even though his word made it clear that he was the only God worthy of worship (Exodus 20:2–6). This, in turn, revealed that his people had forgotten who he was on the most foundational level.

By adding other gods to their worship of the one true God, Israel ceased to worship him altogether.

Conclusion

Ultimately, God's understanding of righteousness and his definitions of sin don't change. Behavior that drove a wedge between him and his created world in biblical times continues to do so today. Likewise, that which brought blessing in biblical times is likely to do so today as well.

The Lord has always rejected the sort of transactional relationship that would make such blessings and curses its focus. However, Scripture is clear that we should not expect our nation—or any nation for that matter—to exist unaffected by how it approaches God's laws.

So, how do Americans treat God's word?

How do we treat each other?

How do we treat God?

How can America's Christians persuade our nation to be a people he can bless?

Let's take a closer look.

SECTION ONE

How do
Americans
relate
to truth?

Introduction

The great twenty-first-century philosopher Pontius Pilate asked, "What is truth?" (John 18:38). Of course, Pilate lived roughly two thousand years ago, but his question still haunts our culture today.

Some have taken it as the launching point for a genuine investigation that ultimately led them to Christ. Unfortunately, many ask his question with the same nihilistic skepticism that plagued Pilate in his confrontation with Jesus.

Similarly, our American culture is so saturated with Christianity in many places that Americans stand face-to-face with the Truth while lamenting its absence.

Our society is not entirely to blame. When the church does not embody the message and relevance of Jesus effectively, many will look at us and struggle to find the face of Christ. They are still responsible for responding to the gospel, of course. But if we want our culture to encounter the Truth, we must be intentional about embracing and displaying it in our lives.

Any progress on a national level must start with Christians demonstrating our respect for the relevance and authority of God's word in how we choose to live. Non-Christians have little reason to value objective truth and biblical authority more highly than we do. If God judges our nation for rejecting his truth, we must be sure that such judgment does not begin with us.

How, then, can we better embody and defend the truth we urgently need to share with the lost around us? Let us now turn to this question.

We will begin with a brief examination of how our culture devolved into a postmodern/post-truth society that seems to have abandoned finding an answer to Pilate's question. We will then look at some of the ways this tragic lack of respect for God's truth has manifested itself in our nation before concluding with what God might think of our culture in this area.

1

A BRIEF HISTORY OF TRUTH: HOW THE TRUTH BECAME "MY TRUTH"

Scripture repeatedly declares that God's word is truth. The psalmist said to God, "All your words are true; all your righteous laws are eternal" (Psalm 119:160). Jesus said to his Father, "Your word is truth" (John 17:17).

He taught us that those who worship God "must worship in the Spirit and in truth" (John 4:24). Our Lord stated clearly, "If you love me, keep my commands" (John 14:15).

When we ignore or disobey God's truth, the consequences are severe.

Samuel asked, "Does the Lord delight in burnt offerings and sacrifices as much as in obeying the Lord?" (1 Samuel 15:22a). Then he stated, "To obey is better than sacrifice, and to heed is better than the fat of rams" (v. 22b).

Moses warned his people that disobeying God's word would lead to devastating curses on their nation (Deuteronomy 28:15–68). Those who reject the word and wisdom of the Lord are in peril of divine judgment (cf. Proverbs 1:24–33).

There are two primary ways to reject the truth of God. One is to deny the existence of truth altogether. The other is to claim that God's word is untruthful.

In this chapter, we will focus on the first. In the following chapter, we will focus on the second.

Aristotle noted that "nature abhors a vacuum." So does culture. Ideas have a history. We think the way we do for a reason—usually, many reasons. Knowing where we've come from is essential to understanding where we are and where we're going. If we are going to change our culture, we must first understand our culture.

A doctor's first step in treating illness is diagnosing it.

In this chapter, we will overview as briefly as possible the history of our culture's rejection of objective truth. We'll see that society's response is not nearly as irrational as many Christians would like to believe but rather the logical conclusion of a world without God. Then we'll explain some reasons why this might actually be good news for the gospel.

Beginning at the beginning

Democracy was a creed before it became a global movement. Communism was a concept in the mind of Karl Marx before it became an ideology that enslaved a third of the world.

Everything we think about ourselves and our world has its origins in movements that began centuries before Jesus. Let's look briefly at our intellectual parents and discover ways they still influence their children today.

Western philosophy began as a reaction to the anthropomorphic ("to make human") religion of the day. Remember Zeus and his cohorts, cavorting around on the top of Mount Olympus and throwing thunderbolts at anyone who displeased them? Remember the gods of Homer's tragic stories, puppet masters who pulled the strings of Greek soldiers and armies for their own amusement? So did the first philosophers, who thought them as absurd as we do.

But why did they ask why?

Six centuries before Christ, a legendary singer-philosopher named

Orpheus changed the world. Orpheus had one principal idea: your soul is an immortal god imprisoned in your body and doomed to reincarnation. He thought that your soul existed in some preincarnate state. But it "sinned," we might say, and was punished by being put into this material world, which was created for just this purgatorial purpose. The world you can see, the flesh you can touch—anything physical at all—is inferior. It is part of this "prison of the soul" and must be escaped.

How? By rituals, ascetic living, and knowledge of the correct magical formula after death. Through the use of a contemplative, rational philosophy, your soul can be purified and released from its abysmal physical jail. Or so Orpheus claimed.

This thought was enlarged by Pythagoras (ca. 570 to ca. 495 BC). If you took high school geometry, perhaps you remember Pythagoras. One of the most famous principles in math is named for him. Pythagoras also invented square numbers and studied musical harmonics. But he did all this in the service of his philosophy and his philosophy in the service of his religion.

Pythagoras and his followers possessed a very strong religious faith rooted in the Orphic cult. They were convinced that their souls had existed in a preincarnate state and must be liberated from the prison house of their bodies through rigorous philosophical thought and right actions. They believed that thought makes the soul divine and that the true universe is a world of order, proportion, harmony, and form. Hence their fascination with mathematics, the only "pure" realm we can know in this fallen life.

So far, Western thinkers focused on a single principle behind the observable universe. This tradition continued with Heraclitus (535 to 475 BC), who argued that change is the unifying principle of the world. He made famous the saying, "You cannot step into the same river twice." He based his views on observation, framing what would become known as "empiricism."

By contrast, Parmenides (born ca. 515 BC) claimed that permanence is the foundational law of the universe. His argument: "That which is is, and it is impossible for it not to be." A = A and cannot be anything else.

Parmenides was the first philosopher to use such purely rational arguments in defense of his ideas. As a result, he is known as the first Rationalist: someone who believes that truth is the result of logical reasoning, not empirical observation. We will meet this worldview many times in the centuries to follow.

Thus, four centuries before Christ, Western thinkers believed that the world could be understood materialistically and that, if the "spiritual" has a place, it is outside and separate from the "secular." Does this sound familiar? From this understanding would emerge the Sophists and the next stage of postmodernism's development.

Truth is what you say it is

Sophists (the word means "wise ones") were pop philosophers, writing how-to handbooks on nearly every subject and traveling around the country conducting seminars and collecting large fees.

In time, the most popular Sophists became international figures in demand all over the Mediterranean world. They advised famous married couples, educated wealthy children, and guided kings and princes. Their services were available to the highest bidder.

Over a single generation, these Sophists became the great celebrities of their culture. They were the first to argue for subjective ethics, the idea that no absolutes exist. According to their philosophy of life, the only wrong idea is the idea that an idea can be wrong.

In time, the Sophists settled on the practice of rhetoric: the art of persuasion by eloquent speech. If no absolute values can be relied upon, the best we can do in life is to convince others that our own subjective ideas are right. The Sophist teachers became brilliant debaters, learning to persuade gigantic crowds of the truth of their chosen ideas. The rest of the intellectual world hated them because, no matter how wrong their positions seemed to be, they could persuade the crowds that they were right.

Socrates, a contemporary of the Sophists, had little patience for their strategy or their philosophy and stood as one of the most important counters to their relativistic view of truth. How did he become so influential? Through two words: "Know thyself."

Socrates argued that the key to knowledge is to acknowledge one's ignorance and then to seek the truth through dialogue. He would seek a definition of the truth in question, test it by common experience, then deduce consequences.

In practice, this method was as maddening as it sounds and earned the great philosopher a reputation as a "gadfly" on the Athenian culture of his day. Ultimately, he would teach our Western civilization that there is an objective truth and that we can know it through personal reasoning and observation (apart from divine revelation or a relationship with God). This belief has functioned as the single most important intellectual foundation for the Western world throughout most of its history.

Socrates' pupil, Plato, would expand upon his assertion to develop an understanding of the world in which everything we see is but a shadow of its more perfect idea existing in another realm. Plato's assertion is especially relevant to our present conversation because of its implications for our view of God.

If Plato is right, we can only know the shadow of who God truly is. Your idea of God may be very different from mine. Who's to say who's right? And what difference does it all make anyway? After all, God will never be more than a vague, unknowable entity who, at best, casts a shadow on our world that merely hints at an otherwise unattainable reality.

Can you see why Greek philosophers had such little interest in personal religion? And why our Western culture has a built-in suspicion of it as well?[8]

In the centuries that followed, many attempted to build on the principles of Socrates and Plato, often coming to completely different conclusions regarding what those principles meant for the best life. The response most relevant to our discussion of postmodernism and the search for truth, however, is that of the Skeptics.

Pyrrho of Elis (ca. 360–270 BC) was their first leader. His argument: Since we cannot know whether our sense perceptions agree with reality, we can never get beyond our senses. So, when our thoughts and our senses conflict, we have no criteria for distinguishing the true from the false. The result: When we suspend all judgment, tranquility will follow. We cannot grasp God or the eternal, and so we should give up our attempts to know them.

Truth in the Age of Enlightenment

Following the time of Socrates and Plato, a great deal of important philosophical and theological development took place, but little of it pertains directly to the issue of characterizing truth.[9] In general, popular thought moved increasingly in the direction of an orthodox reliance upon the Lord and his understanding of truth as revealed in Scripture.

Such an outcome should not be surprising since the Church was the primary entity that guided culture from the mid-300s AD to roughly the dawn of the Enlightenment. While some challenged the orthodox worldview, even dissenting perspectives were often held by those in monasteries among people who remained committed to the Lord.

When Scholasticism reintroduced pagan philosophy to Western culture following the Crusades (beginning in roughly the early to mid-1100s), the vast majority of debates on the nature of truth took place with the intention of better understanding how to account for these new/old ideas in a Christian context.

That began to shift, however, with the Renaissance (roughly 1300 – 1600 AD). Reason became more important than before, as it was shaped through their study of nature and classical literature. Authority structures were deemphasized, the autonomy and enlightenment of humanity were elevated, and concern for the man-man relationship reigned supreme.

In short, for the first time in nearly a millennium, it became acceptable to once again wonder what a world without God might look like. And while few made such a leap at this point, it stimulated some ideas that would come to fruition in the Enlightenment.

The writings of René Descartes (1596–1650) demonstrate an important next step in the shift that would rock our understanding of the nature of truth. Descartes, wanting to offer a rational defense for his beloved and embattled Roman Catholic Church, based his philosophy on the essential principle that "I think, therefore I am." He saw in his ability to rationally observe the world around him the necessary tools to prove not only that God exists but that he is the supreme or absolute being the Church claimed him to be.

In response, John Locke (1632–1704) helped usher in the Empiricist worldview, in which he and others argued that the key to knowledge is not reason but experience. Locke popularized the idea that our minds at birth are "blank slates" upon which experience writes. Knowledge is essentially the sum total of these experiences.

Immanuel Kant (1724–1804) combined these approaches. His essential argument was that our minds contain innate rational categories by which we interpret sensory experience, producing knowledge.

Here's the problem: According to Kant, we cannot know "the thing in itself," only our experience of it. You cannot know the device on which you're reading these words—only what it looks like, sounds like, or feels like. You are limited in your knowledge of reality to your personal, subjective experience as your mind interprets your senses.

This perspective would change the entire course of Western culture.

The path to postmodernism

Those who followed Kant responded to his foundational approach to truth in one of four ways.

Thomas Reid (1710–1796) claimed that common sense allows us to understand our experiences and make self-evident moral judgments. His approach became especially popular in America through the influence of B. B. Warfield and others. As a result, for much of our nation's history, the majority of Americans were satisfied to believe that common sense dictates truth.

The second approach is best epitomized by the Danish philosopher Søren Kierkegaard (1813–1855). Kierkegaard's central tenet was simple: Faith is not intellectual assent but the total commitment of our lives to something. Such commitment is subjective, for its results are not known before they are experienced. Truth is chosen and acted upon.

This passion for the individual's choice and life made Kierkegaard the "father of existentialism." The philosophy attributed to him stresses personal identity and choice as the basis for life. Tragically, there is little place for the community of faith in Kierkegaard's thought or in the school he "founded."

The third approach, and the one most common in our culture today, is that of Friedrich Nietzsche (1844–1900). In brief, Nietzsche agreed with Kant that our language does not reflect reality as such but only our experience of it. For instance, there is no such thing as "leaves," only individual leafs that we experience and synthesize into a universal concept.

Nietzsche claimed that language is purely individual and subjectively the product of our own experiences. As such, language *cannot* reflect a larger, objective reality or truth. This linguistic assertion will be crucial to the further development of postmodernism.

The fourth option is called "pragmatism." Charles Sanders Peirce (1839–1914) helped popularize the idea that truth is "opinion which is fated to be ultimately agreed to by all who investigate." What works for most people will be viewed as true.

The prevailing conclusion was that truth must be individual and subjective. Whether we attain it through common sense, personal experience, linguistic acts, or practical outcomes, the consensus is that truth is what we believe it to be.

Modern postmodernism

This trajectory takes us to the worldview now known as "postmodernism," the claim that all truth is personal and subjective. Three thinkers especially helped define the postmodern understanding of truth with which we live today.

The first was Michel Foucault (1926–1984). Like Nietzsche, he believed that we must reject any claim to objective knowledge and instead focus on the individual and the specific. Consequently, language cannot express universal truth but only the personal experience of its user and/or interpreter.

Jacques Derrida (1930–2004) followed Foucault and expanded upon his understanding of language. Derrida's basic belief was that we "create" our own world by speaking of it. In his view, language possesses no fixed meaning and is not connected to a fixed reality.

For instance, the device on which these words were typed is either a computer, a fancy typewriter, or a strange box that makes annoying clicks depending entirely on whether I (Jim), my grandfather, or my two-year-old grandson are describing it. We cannot get beyond words to the "reality" for words create that reality for us.

As a result, according to Derrida, we should admit the absence of transcendent reality and focus only upon the text itself as it speaks to us personally. Language is not so much a tool for expression as it is one for creation. What our words mean to us is the entirety of their significance, and the same is true for each individual. Consequently, since truth must be expressed in words, there can be no objective truth because everyone serves as their own standard for what that truth would be. This worldview has been enormously influential in the academic world.

Our last thinker is Richard Rorty (1931–2007), one of America's most popular philosophers. While Derrida focused more on the theory of postmodern linguistics, Rorty spent most of his time showing its practical usefulness for our daily lives (at least in his estimation). Because no foundational truths or "first principles" exist apart from our ability to use words to describe them, "truth" is simply our description of the world in a way that works for us.

Rorty believed that such an approach held the capacity to build stronger communities in which people would be more tolerant of others and bring about a kind of postmodern utopia. Before this could happen, however, society must first banish any attempts to require and enforce one particular view of reality and truth over another. Such a postmodern hope offers an enticing, accessible, and nonjudgmental alternative to the Christian worldview built upon a single Way, Truth, and Life.

If you have no desire to accept a biblical understanding of truth or live in accordance with God's will, the kind of society described by Rorty is very appealing. It's not hard to see why so many in our culture have embraced this "tolerant" view of life.

It's also easy to see why so many are willing to withhold the same tolerance toward a Christian worldview that they consider intolerant. These two understandings of truth are incompatible on the most fundamental level. As a result, each person must choose which to follow, a decision that necessitates the rejection of the other.

So how should we proceed? What steps can Christians take to fruitfully and gracefully engage with a worldview that could not be more at odds with our own? What follows is a brief sketch of such an apologetic, approaching an engagement with postmodernism along both philosophical and pragmatic lines.

An apologetic for objective truth

First, a philosophical response. Unfortunately, one approach to postmodernism among Christians is to accept its foundational beliefs and attempt to build a Christian structure upon them. This results in an intensely subjective faith that possesses no intrinsic or objective merit for others. Fortunately, there are other ways.

I suggest that the postmodern rejection of objective truth contains within itself the fissures that may lead to its collapse. In brief, if no objective truth exists, how can I accept this assertion as objectively true? According to postmoderns, no statement possesses independent and objective truth. And yet the preceding statement is held to be independently and objectively true. This seems a bit like the ancient skeptics who claimed, "There is no such thing as certainty and we're sure of it."

A second philosophical critique of postmodernism centers on its rejection of objective ethics. Since all ethics in this view are purely pragmatic and contextual, no ethical position can be judged or rejected by those outside its culture. If this is so, how are we to view events such as the Holocaust? Within the interpretive culture of the Third Reich, Auschwitz and Dachau were pragmatically necessary and purposeful. And yet they stand as the quintessential rejection of the tolerance and inclusion so valued by postmoderns.

There was a time when the postmodern thinker had to choose between his insistence on inclusion and his rejection of intolerance. However, most have come to the basic conclusion today that the one exception to this principle is those who are intolerant of others. Essentially, it's acceptable to be intolerant of intolerance so long as you tolerate everything else.

If, however, our postmodern friend simply shrugs her shoulders and says, "So what?" we can turn to some pragmatic responses. One is to point out the impossibility of living by relative truth. If there are no absolutes, how are we to regulate traffic on our streets? How are parents to discipline their children? How is society to maintain law and order?

A second practical response focuses on the postmodern rejection of objective truth. The chief obstacle to faith posed by modernity was its insistence on empirical proof and scientific verification. The postmodern thinker rejects such a materialist worldview, insisting that all truth claims are equally (though relatively) valid. The result is a renewed interest in spirituality unprecedented in modern times. While this contemporary spirituality is, unfortunately, embracing of all alternatives, at least Christianity can function as one of these options.

How can we make an appeal for biblical authority in such a marketplace of spiritual competitors? By reversing the "modern" strategy. In modernity we told our culture, "Christianity is true; it is therefore relevant and attractive." We invited nonbelievers to accept the faith on the basis of its biblical, objective merits. "The Bible says" was all the authority our truth claims required.

In the postmodern culture, we must use the opposite strategy: our faith must be attractive; then it may be relevant; then it might be true (at least for its followers). If we can show the postmodern seeker of spiritual meaning that Christianity is attractive, interesting, and appealing, he will likely be willing to explore its relevance for his life. When he sees its relevance for us, he may decide to try it for himself. And when it "works," he will decide that it is true for him. He will then affirm the authority of the Scriptures, not in order to come to faith but because he has.

Can such an approach be effective? If we jettison our "truth first" approach to biblical authority and begin by appealing to our culture on the basis of attractive relevance, will we abandon our biblical heritage? No—we will return to it.

We live in a postmodern, post-denominational, post-Christian culture. The first Christians lived in a premodern, pre-denominational, pre-Christian world. They had no hope of taking the gospel to the "ends of the earth" by citing biblical authority to the Gentile culture. The larger Greek world shared the postmodern skepticism of any absolute truth claims, let alone those made on the basis of Hebrew scriptures or a Jewish rabbi's teachings.

As a result, apostolic Christians built their evangelistic efforts on personal relevance and practical ministry. The result was the beginning of the most powerful, popular, and far-reaching religious movement in history.

We are now living in a culture more like that of the apostolic Christians than any we have seen since their day. They had no buildings or institutions to which they could invite a skeptical world, and so they went to that world with the gospel. They had no objective authority base from which to work, so they demonstrated the authority of the Scriptures by their attractive, personal relevance. We now live in a day when nonbelievers will not come to our buildings to listen to our appeals on the basis of biblical authority. But when we show them the pragmatic value of biblical truth in our lives, ministries, and community, we will gain a hearing.

Postmodernity offers us a compelling opportunity to "remember our future." To remember the biblical strategies upon which the Christian movement was founded and to rebuild our ministries on their foundation. To move into our postmodern future on the basis of our premodern heritage.

Every postmodern person I have met wants the same thing: a faith that is practical, loving, and hopeful. The tragedy is that our churches do not always offer them this biblical truth in an attractive and relevant way.

The good news is that we can.

2

THE IMPOTENCE OF SCRIPTURE: WHY "GOD'S WORD SAYS" NO LONGER MATTERS TO OUR CULTURE

Moses commanded God's people to "keep the commands of the Lord your God that I give you" (Deuteronomy 4:2). God told his people that his word "will not return to me empty, but will accomplish what I desire and achieve the purpose for which I sent it" (Isaiah 55:11).

Scripture promises: "Blessed are those whose ways are blameless, who walk according to the law of the Lord. Blessed are those who keep his statutes" (Psalm 119:1–2).

In short, God blesses those who keep his word and judges those who do not.

As we have seen, postmodern skeptics in our post-Christian culture reject biblical authority because they believe all truth claims to be relative, individual, and subjective. For them, no truth source is objectively true—not even the Bible. This rejection of biblical authority jeopardizes all who refuse to accept the truthfulness of God's word.

Others in our secular culture reject biblical truth because they believe the Bible is untrustworthy on its own merits.

For instance, Christopher Hitchens wrote a best seller, *god is not Great: How Religion Poisons Everything*, expressly to undermine the faith of his readers.[10] He claims that the Bible "was put together by crude, uncultured human mammals" and claims in no uncertain terms:

"It can be stated with certainty, and on their own evidence, that the Gospels are most certainly not literal truth."[11]

Clearly, those who claim that God's word cannot be trusted as truth also risk the judgment Scripture predicts (cf. Romans 14:12–13). This rejection raises the question: Can we trust the Bible? Is it truly the authoritative and relevant word of God that it claims to be?

This chapter is intended to equip Christians to answer this question for themselves and their skeptical culture. It also serves as a foundation for the following chapters that discuss moral issues in a biblical context.

Archaeological evidence for the Bible

The lost around us are unlikely to take us at our word when we tell them that the Bible is the trustworthy word of God. Nor should we expect them to. After all, Christians don't agree with Muslims that the Qur'an is a divinely inspired, authoritative mandate for all people. The same is true with the Book of Mormon, the New World Translation of the Holy Scriptures for Jehovah's Witnesses, or any other book that is authoritative for non-Christian religions.

So, what sets the Bible apart? Is there evidence from outside Scripture itself to authenticate it as a book worth believing?

In a word, yes. While there is not archaeological evidence of every person or event found within the Bible, there have been a number of discoveries that help substantiate its historical credibility.

Old Testament discoveries

In 1993, Israeli archaeologists were sifting through debris as they worked on the ruins of the ancient city of Dan in upper Galilee. What they discovered this day would make the front page of the *New York Times*: an inscription, part of a shattered "stele" (monument) that dated to the ninth century before Christ. It commemorated a military victory by the king of Damascus over the king of Israel and the house of David. And it cited the "House of David" clearly and without question.

This was the first non-biblical artifact proving the existence of the great king of Israel. A year later, two other artifacts were discovered naming Jehoram, king of Israel, and Ahaziah, king of Judah. Many scholars now believe that the monument relates to the battle in the region recorded in 2 Chronicles 22:5.

Archaeologists have also discovered dramatic evidence of Solomon's amazing wealth and building campaigns. Fortifications at Hazor, Megiddo, and Gezer date to the middle of the tenth century BC, exactly the time of Solomon's reign. Solomon's "Royal Quarter" has been unearthed in Jerusalem. And part of the Temple he built still stands on the eastern side of the Temple Mount.

Babylonian chronicles of the destruction of Jerusalem precisely parallel the biblical records of this tragic event. And ruins of Nebuchadnezzar's palace complex have been discovered, proving his existence and significant role in the ancient Middle East.

New Testament evidence

According to Luke 3:1, Lysanias was tetrarch of Abilene during the beginning of John the Baptist's ministry. But no evidence of Lysanius' existence had been discovered until an inscription was found which records a temple dedication by him. His name, title, and place all agree with Luke's description.

In 1990, workers building a water park two miles south of the Temple Mount inadvertently broke through the ceiling of a hidden burial chamber. Archaeologists found twelve limestone ossuaries (bone boxes) inside. One of them, decorated with six-petaled rosettes, contained the bones of a sixty-year-old man. It bore the inscription *Yehosef bar Qayafa*, "Joseph son of Caiaphas." Historians have identified the remains as those of the high priest of Jesus' execution.

In 1961, excavations at the seaside ruins of Caesarea Maritima unearthed a first-century inscription. Badly damaged, the Latin inscription reads in part, *Tiberieum . . . [Pon]tius Pilatus . . . [Praef]ectus Juda[ea]e*. The inscription confirms the status of Pontius Pilate as the prefect or governor of Judea.

Yhohnn Yehohanan was a crucifixion victim, executed during the Jewish Revolt in AD 70. His remains were discovered in 1968. His legs were fractured, evidence of the typical Roman means by which death was hastened. Nails were driven through his wrists and heels. His death corresponds precisely with the descriptions of Jesus' crucifixion found in the Gospels (cf. John 19:17–32).

Luke describes Paul's ministry in Corinth and this attack: "While Gallio was proconsul of Achaia, the Jews of Corinth made a united attack on Paul" (Acts 18:12). Gallio ejected Paul's accusers from his court (v. 16) and refused to prosecute Paul. This Gallio is known to be the brother of Seneca, the philosopher, who was himself tutor of Nero. However, critics were skeptical of Luke's claim that Gallio was "proconsul" of Achaia during the time of Paul's ministry there. Then an inscription was discovered at Delphi with this exact title for Gallio; it dates him to AD 51, the precise time Paul was in Corinth.

Erastus is identified in Acts 19:22 as one of Paul's Corinthian coworkers. In excavations in the area of Corinth, we find an inscription which states, "Erastus in return for his aedileship [maintenance of public buildings] laid the pavement at his own expense."

Again, none of these by itself is sufficient to corroborate the whole of the Bible. They do, however, support the fact that Scripture is historically accurate.

Fulfilled prophecy

Jeane Dixon made the news after President Kennedy's assassination when her prediction reported four years earlier in *Parade* magazine was recounted: "As to the 1960 election, Mrs. Dixon thinks it will be dominated by labor and won by a Democrat. But he will be assassinated or die in office, though not necessarily in his first term."

However, in January of 1960, she had claimed, "The symbol of the Presidency is directly over the head of Vice President Nixon." Either he or Democrat John Kennedy had to win the election. Additionally, three of the ten presidents who had served in the twentieth century had died in office, and two others were critically ill at the end of their terms. The odds against her were not as high as we might think.

Further study of psychic claims made in 1975 and observed until 1981 concluded that only six of the seventy-two predictions were fulfilled in any way. A 6 percent accuracy rate is not impressive. [12]

Does the Bible fulfill its predictions? When it makes prophetic statements regarding the future, do they come to pass?

As we consider evidence for biblical authority, we should spend a moment with the fascinating subject of Messianic prophecy and its fulfillment by Jesus Christ. If any book makes promises it does not keep, we are justified in dismissing the rest of its truth claims. But if a book's prophecies rendered centuries earlier are clearly fulfilled in history, we can consider the rest of its claims to be trustworthy as well.

The importance of Messianic prophecy

Jesus repeatedly appealed to Old Testament predictions regarding himself:

- At the beginning of his ministry, he read a Messianic prediction from Isaiah 61, then said to the waiting crowd, "Today this scripture is fulfilled in your hearing" (Luke 4:21).

- He told his critics, "You study the Scriptures diligently because you think that in them you have eternal life. These are the very Scriptures that testify about me, yet you refuse to come to me to have life. . . . If you believed Moses, you would believe me, for he wrote about me" (John 5:39–40, 46).

- At the Last Supper, he warned his disciples, "It is written: 'And he was numbered with the transgressors'; and I tell you that this must be fulfilled in me. Yes, what is written about me is reaching its fulfillment" (Luke 22:37).

- At his arrest, he told the crowd, "This has all taken place that the writings of the prophets might be fulfilled" (Matthew 26:56).

- On Easter Sunday night, he said to the two disciples traveling to Emmaus: "How foolish you are, and how slow to believe all that the prophets have spoken! Did not the Messiah have to suffer these things and then enter his glory?" Then, to explain what he meant, "beginning with Moses and all the Prophets, he explained to them what was said in all the Scriptures concerning himself" (Luke 24:25–26, 27).

- After his resurrection, he said to his astonished disciples, "Everything must be fulfilled that is written about me in the Law of Moses, the Prophets and the Psalms" (Luke 24:44).

New Testament writers made the same appeal, repeatedly claiming that Jesus fulfilled the Old Testament predictions regarding the Messiah:

- At Pentecost, Peter cited prophecies from Joel 2, Psalm 16, and Psalm 110 in claiming that Jesus was the promised Messiah (Acts 2:14–36).

- He later explained Jesus' crucifixion to a crowd at Jerusalem: "This is how God fulfilled what he had foretold through all the prophets, saying that his Messiah would suffer" (Acts 3:18).

- Peter told Cornelius, "All the prophets testify about him that everyone who believes in him receives forgiveness of sins through his name" (Acts 10:43).

- When Paul came to Thessalonica, "As was his custom, [he]

went into the synagogue, and on three Sabbath days he reasoned with them from the Scriptures, explaining and proving that the Messiah had to suffer and rise from the dead. 'This Jesus I am proclaiming to you is the Messiah,' he said" (Acts 17:2–3).

- Paul described his message as "the gospel [God] promised beforehand through his prophets in the Holy Scriptures" (Romans 1:2).

- Paul's message could be summarized: "What I received I passed on to you as of first importance: that Christ died for our sins according to the Scriptures, that he was buried, that he was raised on the third day according to the Scriptures" (1 Corinthians 15:3–4).

Clearly, if Jesus did not fulfill Old Testament predictions regarding the Messiah, both he and his first followers were deceivers of the worst sort. Their movement depended entirely on the claim that he was the promised Messiah of God.

It still does.

Representative Messianic prophecies [13]

More than three hundred times, the Old Testament makes claims or predictions regarding the coming Messiah. Jesus fulfilled every prophecy. Most scholars date Malachi, the last book of the Old Testament, at ca. 400 BC, demonstrating that these predictions were not made during Jesus' day. Translators who created the Septuagint, the Greek Old Testament, began their work ca. 250 BC. At the very least, there were more than two centuries between the last prediction and Jesus' fulfillment.

Listed in order relative to Jesus' earthly life, here are some of the main prophecies to consider:

- Born of a woman's seed (Genesis 3:15 / Galatians 4:4)

- Born of a virgin (Isaiah 7:14 / Matthew 1:18, 24, 25; Luke 1:26–35)

- Descended from Abraham (Genesis 22:18 / Matthew 1:1; Galatians 3:16)

- Descended from Isaac (Genesis 21:12 / Luke 3:23, 34; Matthew 1:2)

- Descended from Jacob (Numbers 24:17 / Luke 3:23, 34)

- Part of the tribe of Judah (Genesis 49:19; Micah 5:2 / Luke 3:23, 33; Matthew 1:2)

- From the family line of Jesse (Isaiah 11:1 / Luke 3:23, 32; Matthew 1:6)

- From the house of David (Jeremiah 23:5 / Luke 3:23, 31; Matthew 1:1)

- Born at Bethlehem (Micah 5:2 / Matthew 2:1)

- Presented with gifts (Psalm 72:10 / Matthew 2:1, 11)

- Children would die (Jeremiah 31:15 / Matthew 2:16)

- Would be anointed by the Spirit (Isaiah 11:2 / Matthew 3:16, 17)

- Preceded by a messenger (Isaiah 40:3; Malachi 3:1 / Matthew 3:1, 2)

- Would minister in Galilee (Isaiah 9:1 / Matthew 4:12, 13, 17)

- Would perform miracles (Isaiah 35:5, 6 / Matthew 9:35)

- Would teach parables (Psalm 78:2 / Matthew 13:34)

- Would enter Jerusalem on a donkey (Zechariah 9:9 / Luke 19:35–37)

- A friend would betray him (Psalm 41:9 / Matthew 10:4)

- Sold for thirty pieces of silver (Zechariah 11:12 / Matthew 26:15)

- Money thrown in the Lord's house (Zechariah 11:13 / Matthew 27:5)

- Money used for a potter's field (Zechariah 11:13 / Matthew 27:7)

- Forsaken by his disciples (Zechariah 13:7 / Mark 14:50)

- Accused by false witnesses (Psalm 35:11 / Matthew 26:59, 60)

- Silent before his accusers (Isaiah 53:7 / Matthew 27:12)

- Wounded and bruised (Isaiah 53:5 / Matthew 27:26)

- Smitten and spit upon (Isaiah 50:6 / Matthew 26:67)

- Mocked (Psalm 22:7, 8 / Matthew 27:29)

- Hands and feet pierced (Psalm 22:16 / Luke 23:33)

- Crucified with thieves (Isaiah 53:12 / Matthew 27:38)

- Prayed for his persecutors (Isaiah 53:12 / Luke 23:34)

- Friends stood afar off (Psalm 38:11 / Luke 23:49)

- Garments parted and lots cast (Psalm 22:18 / John 19:23, 24)

- Would suffer thirst (Psalm 69:21 / John 19:28)

- Gall and vinegar offered (Psalm 69:21 / Matthew 27:34)

- Would be forsaken by God (Psalm 22:1 / Matthew 27:46)

- Would commit himself to God (Psalm 31:5 / Luke 23:46)

- No bones broken (Psalm 34:20 / John 19:33)

- His side pierced (Zechariah 12:10 / John 19:34)

- Buried in a wealthy man's tomb (Isaiah 53:9 / Matthew 27:57–60)

- Would be raised from the dead (Psalm 16:10 / Acts 2:31)

- Would ascend to heaven (Psalm 68:18 / Acts 1:9)

- Would be seated at the right hand of God (Psalm 110:1 / Hebrews 1:3)

What are the chances that one person could fulfill each of these predictions? Many of them were beyond Jesus' human control, such as the soldier's decision to thrust his spear into Jesus' side.

Were they coincidental? Mathematician Peter Stoner once calculated the odds of one man's fulfillment of just eight of these predictions: one in ten to the seventeenth power (one followed by seventeen zeroes). That number would fill the state of Texas two feet deep in silver dollars. Stoner then considered forty-eight of the Messianic prophecies and determined their odds to be one in ten to the 157th power.

Clearly, the Bible keeps its promises. And its central figure is who he claimed to be: the Messiah of God.

A respectful reading of the Bible

Simply believing the Bible to be true, however, only shows respect for God's word if Scripture also has an impact on our lives. That impact comes from engaging with Scripture in a personal and intentional manner.

We may believe that the Bible is divinely inspired and that it stands up to every test and critique from a skeptical world, but if we do not put its truths into practice, our beliefs ring hollow. To convince our secular culture that Scripture is true, we must personally live out its truths.

So, how can we approach God's word in a way that shows respect to its Author while providing the greatest impact on our lives and service? Taking the proper approach to reading Scripture is a vital place to start.

Personal preparations

We will focus now on what is known as "general hermeneutics." Hermes was the messenger god; hermeneutics is therefore the study of a message or principles of interpretation. Biblical hermeneutics is the field of study that identifies necessary rules and guidelines for Bible study.

Before we can use such principles, however, we must first make three personal commitments. Because the Bible is God's word, not merely the product of human knowledge and study, we must be ready spiritually to hear what it says to us.

First, you must *know the Author of this book personally.*

Paul warned the Corinthians, "The person without the Spirit does not accept the things that come from the Spirit of God but considers them foolishness, and cannot understand them because they are discerned only through the Spirit" (1 Corinthians 2:14). When the lost claim that the Bible is irrelevant to a particular subject, know that they do so because they are, in many ways, incapable of thinking otherwise.

Second, *be willing to work hard.*

Paul challenged his young apprentice in the ministry: "Devote yourself to the public reading of Scripture, to preaching and to teaching" (1 Timothy 4:13). "Devote yourself" translates a Greek term which requires previous, private preparations. Like any area of intellectual investigation, understanding and applying the Scriptures requires personal work. The more you invest, the greater the return.

Ministry students sometimes tell me (Jim) they want to pastor a "New Testament church." I always ask them which one. I'd enjoy pastoring in Antioch, not so much in Corinth. According to Paul, one of the Corinthian problems was their immaturity: "Brothers and sisters, I could not address you as people who live by the Spirit but as people who are still worldly—mere infants`in Christ. I gave you milk, not solid food,`for you were not yet ready for it.`Indeed, you are still not ready." (1 Corinthians 3:1–3). Milk is food digested by a mother and made palatable for her child. Unfortunately, the Corinthians wanted their spiritual truth the same way—digested by someone else.

Many Christians suffer from the Corinthian desire to let others study Scripture for them. "That's what we pay a pastor for," they say. "I've not been to seminary. I don't have time to study the Bible. So, I'll listen to my minister or Sunday school teacher. I'll let the professionals do it."

But the Bible is meant for every believer. You are privileged and responsible to interpret God's word for yourself. If we want to help our culture understand why Scripture is worthy of their respect, we must show them that we respect it first. The lost will never have as much interaction with God's word as with his people.

Third, *obey what you discover*.

The Bible is not meant to inform our minds so much as it intends to change our lives. Jesus said, "Anyone who chooses to do the will of God will find out`whether my teaching comes from God or whether I speak on my own" (John 7:17). Obedience leads to relationship. Faith is required. We must position ourselves to receive what God wants to give by grace. The Israelites had to step into the flooded Jordan River before God would stop its flow (Joshua 3:15–16).

Decide before you open God's word that you will obey what you find there. Write your Father a blank check of obedience. He will not reveal his will as an option to consider but as an ordinance to follow. If you will not do what he says, you'll not understand what he says.

Guiding presuppositions

My high school geometry class acquainted me with the concept of "axioms." These are unprovable presuppositions, guiding beliefs that are basic to the study of mathematics.

For example, we cannot prove that parallel lines never intersect, so we accept by faith that this principle is true in the study of geometry.

All knowledge is built on such presuppositions. Scientists believe the physical universe to be stable and predictable; otherwise, experiments could never be repeated. If Zeus and his cohort change the composition of water every day, marine biologists are in trouble.

Bible study is built on certain presuppositions as well. Four are especially important to our interpretation of God's word.

First, *believe that you can understand Scripture*.

Luther and the Reformers were adamant that the Bible could be understood. God has given us his revelation in such a way that we can discover and apply its truths. We need not depend on creeds, councils, and church tradition. Every believer is his or her own priest before God and his word. While this does not mean that every interpretation is correct, it does mean that every believer is ultimately responsible for his or her engagement with Scripture.

Second, *use the New Testament to interpret the Old*.

Scripture exists to lead us to faith in Jesus (John 20:30–31). The New Testament, which reveals Christ, is therefore our means of interpreting the Old Testament, which prepares the way for him. As Jesus said repeatedly, he fulfills the Scriptures that told the world of his coming.

In other words, we should study Scripture according to the theological doctrine of "progressive revelation." We believe that God reveals himself progressively, building later revelation upon earlier truth.

As a mathematics teacher must teach arithmetic before she can teach geometry and teach trigonometry before she can discuss calculus, so God reveals himself progressively to us. Upon the foundation of the Law, God spoke through his prophets. They, in turn, focused on the Messiah, God's personal revelation. The New Testament builds on this revelation in a Person through revelation in words. The New Testament is therefore God's fullest revelation of himself to us and our means of interpreting his earlier revelation.

This guiding presupposition leads to an important principle: whenever an Old Testament law is renewed in the New Testament, it retains the force of law for Christians today. For instance, by endorsing the Ten Commandments, Jesus made them obligatory for his followers (Matthew 19:16–19).

On the other hand, any Old Testament law not renewed in the New Testament retains the force of principle for Christian living. For instance, the Jewish dietary codes were made nonbinding on Gentile converts by the Jerusalem Council (Acts 15:28–29). However, these laws still demonstrate the relevant principle that God cares about our physical health. We will study them to discover principles and truths that apply to our lives as we relate to God through grace.

Third, *make the Bible its own commentary.*

Our third guiding presupposition is that the Scriptures interpret themselves. Because God's word is unified, coherent, and fully inspired, every word is the word of God. And so, the best way to study any single passage is to interpret it in light of the rest of the Bible. We should seek to compare Scripture with Scripture, interpreting the part by the whole.

Five important principles emerge from this presupposition:

- *Interpret unclear passages in light of clear truth.* Study the difficult parts of Scripture in light of its clear teachings.

- *Do not base doctrine on only one text.* For instance, consider the "millennium," found explicitly only in Revelation 20:1–6. This is obviously an important subject, but it should not be made a test of orthodoxy. At least seven theories on the subject are held by Bible-believing scholars. No person's belief in biblical authority should be questioned because of his or her theory on the millennium. We should seek to build major doctrines on more extensive biblical texts.

- *Study brief passages in light of longer texts.* Interpret a single verse in light of the larger passage in which it is found, that passage in light of its book, and the book in light of the entire Bible. As you consider the larger counsel of God's word, you will allow Scripture to interpret itself.

- *Apply doctrine taught in various parts of Scripture to all times and cultures.* There are a variety of contexts and circumstances behind the various passages of God's word. Whenever a statement is found in a number of different contexts and is taught by a variety of biblical authors, we may know that it was intended as a timeless statement of truth. If it is taught only by one author in one place, we can know that it was a specific statement for that time and context. It will apply in principle to our lives, but perhaps not in precept. In this sense, it is like an Old Testament law not renewed in the New Testament: it teaches spiritual truth but not binding obligation.

- *If two biblical statements appear humanly to contradict, accept both.* Divine truth is not bound by human logic and often must be expressed by two statements that appear to contradict each other. This is known as "antinomy," the acceptance of two principles which seem mutually exclusive but are each independently true.

Last, we must always remember to ask the question, "What was the author's purpose?" Writing in the ancient world was too hard to do without a compelling purpose. Today we drop a note in the mail or send an email in a moment. Ancient writers paid a high price to produce the biblical books we read today.

As a result, we need to know all we can about the author's intended purpose before we try to interpret his writing. Much of Scripture is "task theology," produced to accomplish a specific task or purpose. If we don't understand the task at hand, we'll miss much of what the writer wants us to know and do.

For example, consider the purpose for which John wrote his gospel: "Jesus performed many other signs`in the presence of his disciples, which are not recorded in this book. But these are written that you may believe that Jesus is the Messiah, the Son of God,`and that by believing you may have life in his name" (John 20:30 – 31).

John wants to lead his readers to trust Jesus as their Messiah so that they might find "life in his name." We would expect to find numerous signs and evidences of Jesus' divinity and examples of the transforming power of his love. And that's exactly what John gives us.

This principle is also important for understanding how to discern the primary purpose of a passage that could be used in multiple ways. For example, the Bible begins with an account of God's creation in Genesis 1 and 2. A great deal of ink and metaphorical blood has been spilled over the degree to which those chapters should be read scientifically, historically, allegorically, etc. In the process, many have missed that the primary purpose of the passage is not so much to tell us how God created the world but why.

People can take multiple perspectives on the degree to which that passage must be read literally while still respecting God's truth. The truths of primary importance are that it was God who did the creating and that he did so because he loved us. When Christians accuse other Christians of disrespecting God's word because they disagree on the nonessentials, however important they might otherwise be, we jeopardize our witness to the non-Christian world.

Conclusion

Clearly, there is sufficient historical and textual evidence to demonstrate that Scripture is trustworthy. Christians can and should feel confident that their respect for the Bible as a truthful record of God's truth is well placed.

At the same time, we should not be surprised when those who do not know Christ fail to share our confidence.

As a result, it is vital that believers think and live biblically. We are the only Bible non-Christians are likely to read. Like the moon reflects the sun at night, so we are to reflect the Son in our dark culture.

When others read your life today, what—or Whom—will they find?

3

THE TOLERANCE OF UNBIBLICAL SEXUALITY: HOW THE LGBTQ AGENDA VIOLATES GOD'S WILL

In previous chapters, we examined the reasons why our secular culture believes that truth is subjective and God's word is neither absolute nor trustworthy. Now we will turn to some of the consequences of rejecting objective morality and biblical truth.

Human sexuality is not the only topic we could consider, but it is so powerful and pervasive in human experience that it deserves our attention and response.

In this chapter, we will discuss sexual activity that is forbidden by God's word. In the next chapter, we will explore gender norms and the tolerance of unbiblical lifestyles.

Sinful sexuality

God's word repeatedly calls us to sexual purity. In short, all sexual activity outside the covenant marriage of one man and one woman is unbiblical. When we violate God's will, we must face his judgment.

Sexual behavior that violates biblical norms is the product of rejecting biblical authority. Unfortunately, many in the evangelical world focus primarily on homosexuality and related issues. However, homosexual activity is by no means the only, or even the most common, way our culture exhibits such behavior. This fact is true for Christians as well as for nonbelievers.

It is therefore vital that we stand against all sexual activity outside of the biblical marriage covenant. If we focus only on homosexual activity, we risk losing credibility with our culture. This is especially true for younger generations. As the Pew Research Center found, almost twice as many evangelicals born after 1964 now support same-sex marriage when compared to those born before 1964. Similar trends hold across Christian denominations. [14]

The current direction continues trends that began with the sexual revolution of the 1960s and 1970s. There were Christians who opposed that movement then, just as there are those who oppose the legalization and acceptance of same-sex marriage today.

Overall, however, it seems that in the first stages of the sexual revolution, many in younger generations were not influenced by the church's message on biblical sexual morality. As their generation grew older and took over the leadership of churches and families today, acceptance of sex outside of marriage became more entrenched in the Christian culture.

The acceptance of same-sex marriage, and homosexual activity in general, was the next logical step. Why should heterosexual sex outside of marriage be permissible but homosexual sex be forbidden when the Bible clearly condemns both, often in the same sentence (1 Corinthians 6:9–11)? If Scripture's stance on the former is outdated or irrelevant, why would the same not be true of the latter?

The hypocrisy in condemning one but not the other removes much of the foundation upon which any biblical argument against the acceptance of same-sex marriage must be built. The larger culture, and even other believers, have little reason to listen when we tell them that Scripture's view of homosexual activity is correct if we isolate that sin to the exclusion of other sins.

While it's important to defend God's view of homosexual activity, it's equally important to teach and obey the full counsel of Scripture regarding *all* sexual activity. People deserve to know God's plan for their lives, but far too often that plan is obscured by the hypocrisy and failings of his people.

Ultimately, whether people accept or reject God's truth is up to them, but they deserve to see Christians living out that truth faithfully. The One who made us knows what is best for us, and his word provides guideposts to keep us safely on the road of his perfect will (Romans 12:2).

So, what does his word say on this subject?

A biblical view of sex outside of marriage

We begin our discussion with an examination of the Bible's teachings on the subject of sex outside of marriage, whether it be heterosexual or homosexual in nature.

Paul advised the Corinthians, "But since sexual immorality is occurring, each man should have sexual relations with his own wife, and each woman with her own husband" (1 Corinthians 7:2). The Greek word translated "sexual immorality" is *porneia*, from which we get "pornography." It referred to all forms of immoral sexual activity, from premarital and extramarital sex to prostitution.

In our text, Paul clearly taught that men and women should not engage in sexual relations before they are married, referring to such behavior as "sexual immorality." If sex before marriage was permissible, why would the apostle issue this injunction?

Hebrews 13:4 adds, "Marriage should be honored by all, and the marriage bed kept pure, for God will judge the adulterer and all the sexually immoral." Here again, "sexually immoral" (*pornos*) refers to all immoral sexual activity, including sex outside of marriage.

The Jerusalem council encouraged Gentile Christians to abstain from "sexual immorality" (Acts 15:20). "Sexual immorality" is listed among the "acts of the flesh" (Galatians 5:19). In 1 Thessalonians 4:3,

Paul taught, "It is God's will that you should be sanctified: that you should avoid sexual immorality."

Additionally, when Jesus describes marriage in Matthew 19:4–6, he quotes Genesis 2:24 on how two people become one flesh in marriage. The basic idea is that sex unites people in a way that is only fitting for the kind of lifelong commitment seen in marriage. Paul expounds upon that idea in 1 Corinthians 6:16 when he declares that anyone who "unites himself with a prostitute is one with her in body." Sex joins people in a spiritual and emotional way that is not meant to be broken.

One more fact: many Old Testament figures did not live by God's "one woman and one man" intention for marriage, but Scripture often shows how their sexual sins led to significant consequences in their lives. For instance, Jacob had twelve sons with four women; his family was one of the most dysfunctional in Scripture. David's sin with Bathsheba stained his reputation for all time. Solomon's many wives led him into horrific immorality and idolatry (1 Kings 11).

The biblical teaching is clear: all sex outside of marriage is sinful and carries with it a host of consequences that often prove catastrophic for those who fail to heed God's truth on the subject.

While Scripture is clear that sex is only meant for the marriage covenant, the question remains as to why that covenant must only be between a husband and wife. Why is it still sinful for two people of the same gender to engage in sexual activity if they first entered into a similarly committed relationship? Is God's word on this subject still relevant in a time where such relationships are increasingly accepted in our culture?

What does the Bible say about homosexual activity?

Here's the short version: the Bible teaches that homosexual activity is wrong, but this sin is not unforgivable, and God loves every person he's created—LGBTQ people included. This position usually angers both sides of the argument. Those who affirm homosexuality obviously disagree with it. And many who agree that the Bible condemns homosexual activity want to condemn homosexuals as well, a sentiment the Bible strongly rejects.

Our purpose in this section is not to give you our opinion but God's, as objectively and fairly as we can. This book is written from the perspective that the Bible is the timeless truth of God. As I (Jim) have taught principles of biblical interpretation at seminaries over the years, I have often told my students, "The Bible can never mean what it never meant." We should always seek the intended meaning of the text. I have also said often, "The only word God is obligated to bless is his word." We are not writing to tell you what we think, but to give you God's position on the subject as we—and the vast majority of Christians throughout the church's history—understand it.

Sodom: Gone but not forgotten

The Supreme Court made history on June 27, 2003, when it struck down the "sodomy laws" of the state of Texas. In a 6–3 decision, the justices reversed a ruling made seventeen years earlier that allowed states to punish homosexuals for private consensual sex. Such activity is typically called "sodomy" because of the biblical story we'll now explore.

A man named Lot entertained two angels who came to his city to investigate its sins. These angels came in the physical appearance of men. Before they went to bed, "all the men from every part of the city of Sodom—both young and old—surrounded the house. They called to Lot, 'Where are the men who came to you tonight? Bring them out to us so that we can have sex with them'" (Genesis 19:4–5). For this sin, "the Lord rained down burning sulfur on Sodom" (v. 24), destroying the city.

Is this text a condemnation of homosexuality today? How many well-meaning Christians and scholars have answered that question reveals the dangers of taking a postmodern approach to interpreting the Bible.

Scholar Walter Wink, for example, said no. He believes the passage references a gang rape in Sodom and was "a case of ostensibly heterosexual males intent on humiliating strangers by treating them 'like women,' thus demasculinizing them."[15] However, Dr. Wink offered no biblical evidence that the men were "ostensibly heterosexual." His guess is not shared by the majority of scholars who have studied the story.

The late Dr. Peter Gomes, onetime minister at Harvard's Memorial Church and Plummer Professor of Christian Morals in Harvard College, offered a different approach. He wrote an introduction to the Bible and its message, *The Good Book*. Dr. Gomes, himself a homosexual, viewed this passage as an attempted homosexual rape and argued that it does not condemn homosexuality per se.[16]

A third approach was suggested by D. Sherwin Bailey in his influential book, *Homosexuality and the Western Christian Tradition*. Dr. Bailey believed that the Hebrew word for "know," translated "have sex" by the New International Version, should be translated "show hospitality" instead. He noted that the word appears more than 943 times in the Old Testament and only twelve times in the context of sexual activity.[17]

However, ten of these twelve occurrences are in the book of Genesis, the setting for our story. Lot offered his daughters to the men so they could "do what you like with them" (Genesis 19:8). Apparently, he understood their desires as sexual. Everett Fox's excellent translation of Genesis includes the note, "the meaning is unmistakably sexual." And Jude 7 settles the question as to whether sexual activity is meant in our story: "Sodom and Gomorrah and the surrounding towns gave themselves up to sexual immorality and perversion."[18]

Many interpreters throughout Jewish and Christian history have understood the "sin of Sodom" as homosexuality—not attempted rape—and have viewed God's punishment of Sodom and Gomorrah as his sentiment about all gay people. But I'm not sure their position is justified. Without a doubt, the men of Sodom wanted to have sex with the "men" who had come to their city. But it is also clear that they would have assaulted these visitors to do so.

In short, the sin of Sodom is clearly attempted homosexual rape. However, those who argue for committed, monogamous homosexual relations are right in stating that Genesis 19 does not specifically address such relationships.

Leviticus: Outdated legalism?

Leviticus 18:22 is much less ambiguous: "Do not have sexual relations with a man as one does with a woman; that is detestable." The Hebrew original is as clear as the English translation.

The obvious sense of the command seems to be that homosexual sexual relations are forbidden by Scripture. This is the way the text has typically been understood by Jewish and Christian interpreters across the centuries. It is still the way most read the text today.

But those who advocate homosexuality as an acceptable biblical lifestyle have found ways to dissent. Dr. Wink admitted that this text "unequivocally condemn[s] same-sex sexual behavior."[19] But he theorized that the ancient Hebrews saw any sexual activity which could not lead to the creation of life as a form of abortion or murder. He added that the Jews would have seen homosexuality as alien or pagan behavior.

He then cited the penalty for homosexual behavior: "If a man has sexual relations with a man as one does with a woman, both of them have done what is detestable. They are to be put to death" (Leviticus 20:13). In his reasoning, if we see this punishment for homosexuality as obsolete today, we should see the prohibition of this behavior as equally outdated.

Other scholars suggest that these laws expressed worship codes binding only on Hebrew priests, not universal moral standards. And they connect them with kosher dietary regulations and other rules which they view as intended only for the ancient world.

Is there an objective way to respond to these assertions?

First, let's consider the claim that this Old Testament law has no relevance for New Testament believers. A basic rule of biblical interpretation is that any Old Testament teaching repeated in the New Testament is still binding on the Christian church and faith.[20] As we will see, prohibitions against homosexuality are as clear in the New Testament as in the Old. Even those Old Testament statements that are not repeated in the New Testament carry the force of principle; for instance, kosher laws tell us that God cares about our health.

Second, let's respond to the view that the Leviticus passages related only to the priests and not the larger community. Note that the chapter in question begins, "The Lord said to Moses, 'Speak to the people of Israel and say to them'" (18:1–2). Nothing in the chapter limits its application to the priests. In fact, it prohibits incest, child sacrifice, and sexual relations with beasts—moral standards most people would consider universal.

Third, let's deal with the Leviticus mandate that homosexuals are to be executed (Leviticus 20:13). If we no longer execute those who practice homosexuality, aren't we justified in ignoring this prohibition against such activity?

No one I know would argue that homosexual practice should result in the death penalty today. But note that this law was given to Israel at a crucial time in her early formation. The nation had no court system. Her moral character was not yet formed. And so, the Lord gave the nation clear and enforceable standards that would help solidify and preserve her spiritual future. The spirit of the prohibition is clear: homosexuality is not to be practiced or accepted by the nation.

Also note that reinterpreting the penalty does not mean that we ignore the law. Leviticus also prescribes the death penalty for child sacrifice (20:2), adultery (v. 10), and bestiality (vs. 15–16). I presume we would not accept these practices as moral and lawful today on the basis that the Leviticus punishment for them is not prosecuted by our society.

To sum up, these two passages in Leviticus seem clearly to forbid homosexual activity in any form. But what of the New Testament? Is God's prohibition of homosexual activity still in effect after Jesus came to establish a new covenant and enable us to have a new relationship with the Lord?

What about New Testament grace?

I grew up with a mental image of two gods: the Old Testament Judge of wrath and the New Testament Father of love. The Old Testament Judge might condemn sin, but the New Testament Father loves his kids. Christians live by New Testament grace. Even if the Old Testament consistently teaches that homosexuality is wrong, we should view such legalism in the light of Christian mercy and love—or so some say.

Except that the New Testament is as consistent on this issue as the Old and even more explicit.

Let's begin with Romans 1:26–27: "God gave them over` to shameful lusts.`Even their women exchanged natural sexual relations for unnatural ones.`In the same way the men also abandoned natural relations with women and were inflamed with lust for one another. Men committed shameful acts with other men, and received in themselves the due penalty for their error."

It seems clear that Paul believed homosexuality to be wrong, doesn't it? Not to everyone. Consider four responses by those who would seek to reinterpret God's truth on the subject.

One: Paul was addressing heterosexual men and women who chose homosexual activity, which would, of course, be "unnatural" for them. If this is true, Paul's statement bears no relevance to those who consider themselves homosexual by innate or "natural" orientation.

However, Paul described homosexual acts as "shameful lusts" (v. 26) and "shameless acts" (v. 27). To suggest that his descriptions relate only to the (supposed) decision to engage in such activity by heterosexuals is to strain the Greek syntax beyond its meaning. Nothing in the text suggests that it relates only to heterosexuals.

And he stated that men who engaged in homosexual activity "abandoned natural relations with women," making clear the fact that he considered heterosexuality to be "natural." Likewise, he described lesbian activity as "unnatural."

Two: The "exploitative option" suggests that Paul had in view men who sexually oppress other men (via pederasty, prostitution, master-slave sex, etc.) rather than through consensual, loving relations. The Genesis 19 gang-rape story is (supposedly) an example of the behavior he forbade.

However, the apostle's statement that men "inflamed with lust for one another" shows that he had consensual relations in mind, not just exploitative acts. In addition, Paul included lesbians; there are no examples in his day of women being sexually exploited by other women.

Three: Paul was rejecting behavior at the Roman imperial court, which was infamous for its gross sexual immoralities. By extension, he argued that God's people are to be different from their culture.

However, the apostle nowhere limited his discussion to the imperial court or even to Roman culture and context.

Four: Paul was unaware of innate homosexual orientation and thus addressed homosexual acts as "unnatural."

However, the apostle addressed "lusts" (v. 26), the expression of sexual orientation. Thus, he was clearly aware of orientation and did not convey ignorant or misleading principles in this regard. Paul was a biblical writer inspired by the Holy Spirit (2 Timothy 3:16; 2 Peter 3:15–16). If he did not understand innate homosexual orientation and thus was wrong in addressing homosexuality as he did, we are left to wonder where else the Bible has misled us for twenty centuries.

The next passage to consider is 1 Corinthians 6:9–10: "Do you not know that wrongdoers will not inherit the kingdom of God?`Do not be deceived:`Neither the sexually immoral nor idolaters nor adulterers`nor men who have sex with men nor thieves nor the greedy nor drunkards nor slanderers nor swindlers`will inherit the kingdom of God."

"Men who have sex with men" are clearly among those considered "wrongdoers" by Paul. This phrase is translated from two Greek words: *malakoi* and *arsenokoitei*. The first is a technical term for the passive partner in homosexual activity; the second seems to have been coined by Paul. As we will see, some claim that it refers to economic exploitation, not sexual behavior. As a result, it is possible to interpret the phrase as prohibiting homosexual prostitution, not loving, monogamous homosexual relations.

However, *arsenokoitei* is derived from the Greek translation of Leviticus 20:13, which employs *arsenos koiten:* "a male having sexual relations" with another male. Clearly, Paul had this prohibition against homosexual sexual relations in mind.

The last passage often cited in this discussion is from part of Paul's first letter to Timothy. Here is the paragraph in which our verse is found: "We know that the law is good`if one uses it properly. We also know that the law is made not for the righteous`but for lawbreakers and rebels,`the ungodly and sinful, the unholy and irreligious, for those who kill their fathers or mothers, for murderers, for the sexually immoral, for those practicing homosexuality, for slave traders and liars and perjurers—and for whatever else is contrary to the sound doctrine that conforms to the gospel concerning the glory of the blessed God, which he entrusted to me" (1 Timothy 1:8–11).

The phrase in question is found in verse 10, translated by the ESV as "men who practice homosexuality." The phrase is translated from the Greek *arsenokoites*. As we saw above, it was coined by Paul to refer to men who have sexual relations with men.

Common questions

Assuming we view the Bible as objectively true and agree with its prohibition against homosexual behavior, we need to address some questions commonly asked by those who disagree with us. After all, the majority of those who disagree with the biblical view of homosexual activity, and, by extension, sexual sin of other kinds, will not simply accept Scripture's authority on the topic if it disagrees with what makes the most sense to them.

As discussed in the chapter on postmodernism, this appeal to common sense remains one of the most important tools in discerning the truth for the majority of our nation today. If forced to choose between a clear teaching of Scripture and an interpretation that, while stretched, better fits with what they would prefer to believe, many will choose the latter. As a result, it is vital that our understanding of this subject not only adheres to biblical standards but also that it does not go beyond them.

To that end, we will now turn to some common questions and misconceptions about what Scripture teaches regarding homosexuality and homosexual activity.

Can homosexuals be Christians?

Paul lists people who engage in homosexual activity among those who "will not inherit the kingdom of God" (1 Corinthians 6:9). However, such activity is not the "unpardonable sin." If homosexuality keeps a person from salvation, so does theft, greed, drunkenness, slander, and swindling (other sins listed in the same text). There is no sin God cannot forgive for those who accept his pardon (Isaiah 43:25).

Nowhere does the Bible state that we must repent of specific sins before we can receive salvation. Once the Holy Spirit comes to dwell in us, he will lead us to further repentance and consecration.

If God is love, why would he be against two people loving each other in a monogamous relationship?

It is clear that "God is love" (1 John 4:8), but it does not follow that he is the author of every relationship that claims to be loving. His word warns against adultery, for instance (Exodus 20:14). Incest and polygamy are wrong, even if those who engage in them claim to do so out of love. It is the same for same-sex partners, even if they remain monogamous.

Another point should be made here: Scripture forbids homosexual activity, not homosexual orientation. All sex outside of biblical marriage is wrong, whether heterosexual or homosexual. The sin is not in being attracted to a person of the same sex, or even loving that person. The sin is in expressing that attraction sexually.

Does God make a homosexual a homosexual?

What about the argument that homosexuality is inherited? If this is true, at least for some, how can such an orientation be wrong? "God made me this way" is the testimony of many homosexuals. Did God make a mistake? Or have we misunderstood his word on the issue?

The connection between genetics and homosexuality is tenuous at best. Some researchers have claimed to discover a physical or genetic propensity toward homosexual orientation, but others have refuted their conclusions. Investigations of physical characteristics (such as the size of the hypothalamus, the most famous such study) are inconclusive at best.

According to the American Psychological Association,

> There is no consensus among scientists about the exact reasons that an individual develops a heterosexual, bisexual, gay, or lesbian orientation. Although much research has examined the possible genetic, hormonal, developmental, social, and cultural influences on sexual orientation, no findings have emerged that permit scientists to conclude that sexual orientation is determined by any particular

factor or factors. Many think that nature and nurture both play complex roles; most people experience little or no sense of choice about their sexual orientation.[21]

It is widely believed that alcoholism can be an inherited genetic propensity, but no one would therefore endorse its practice. This fact is emphatically not meant to equate alcoholism and homosexuality. Rather, it is intended to illustrate the fact that not every genetic tendency should be endorsed (if homosexuality is, in fact, such a genetic tendency).

If, however, people are homosexual completely apart from their own decision, it seems to me that they have a right to ask about the fairness of God. If his word teaches that homosexuality is wrong, yet they are homosexual through no choice of their own, how can God be fair in condemning what he seems to have permitted? We will discuss this question further below.

Is homosexuality due to nature or nurture?

What about family and environment? Studies have focused on identical twins who were separated at birth, where one developed a homosexual orientation but the other did not. Some believe that specific family or circumstantial patterns contribute to a child's sexual orientation. In particular, the absence of a strong father and/or the presence of a dominating mother is often noted in families that produce homosexual children. And so, it is claimed that the children of such environments had no choice in their sexual orientation.

It would be difficult to prove this connection, of course. What about heterosexual children produced by the same family environments? Even if family conditions are related to sexual orientation, such a connection does not endorse behavior any more than an abusive parent is justified by the fact that he was the child of an abusive parent.

Homosexuals seem to fall into two categories. I have known some who can remember decisions, choices, and circumstances by which they moved into this lifestyle. I have known others who believe that their orientation existed from birth or prior to conscious choice. It is obviously both impossible and wrong for me to say which category is appropriate to a specific person. But whether homosexuality is a choice or not, this issue does not determine its validity as a lifestyle according to the word of God.

Why would God forbid homosexuality?

Those who explore the biblical position on any ethical issue should also ask why the Scriptures advocate the doctrine they teach. Why would the Lord of the universe take sides on the question of our personal sexual orientation and lifestyle? Many say that so long as we're not hurting others or ourselves, our personal consensual acts should be private and permitted.

Except that homosexual behavior *does* hurt many who participate in it.

A study in the United Kingdom reported that homosexuals are about 50 percent more likely to suffer from depression and engage in substance abuse than the rest of the population. They are also 200 percent more likely to be at risk for suicide. [22]

According to the National Lesbian Health Care Survey, over half the sample had had thoughts about suicide at some time, and 18 percent had attempted suicide. About three-fourths had received counseling at some time, half for reasons of sadness and depression. [23]

A typical response to these studies is that gays and lesbians in the US live in a homophobic culture, and that increasing acceptance of their lifestyles would mitigate these risks. However, homosexuals in Denmark, a culture that is highly tolerant of homosexuality, die as early as those in the US—on average, in their early fifties (or in their early forties if AIDS is the cause of death). [24] The Centers for Disease Control and Prevention reports that men who have sex with men constitute 2 percent of the US population, but accounted for more than half of all estimated new HIV infections annually from 2008 to 2010. [25]

Some homosexuals do commit themselves to lifelong, monogamous, apparently healthy relationships. Unfortunately, this is more the exception than the rule. *The Journal of Sex Research* found that "the modal range for number of [homosexual] sexual partners ever was 101–500." In other words, the number of participants in the study reporting 101–500 sexual partners was higher than any other group. [26]

I mean no unkindness or disrespect in commenting on the issue of homosexuality and emotional or physical health. My point is simply that our Father has a reason for his word on the issue. His concern is for his children and our well-being. There is a purpose behind his position on our subject.

But if homosexual activity is sinful and harmful, why would God permit it in the first place?

Why does God permit homosexuality?

It is clear that our Father warns us against homosexual activity, given the ways it can hurt his children. So, we can answer the question: Does God make people gay? Clearly not. A holy God could not intend people to possess attributes or characteristics he condemns. Why, then, are some people homosexual?

You and I inherited a sin nature (Romans 5:12). That sin nature shows up in a variety of ways. What tempts me might not tempt you and vice versa. You could lock me in a liquor store and I'd leave tomorrow as sober as I am right now. I'm not bragging—it's just a fact that nothing in my nature pushes me toward alcohol and alcoholism. However, my alcoholic friends probably don't struggle with my temptations any more than I share theirs.

Unfortunately, God must permit these problems and conditions as a consequence of the Fall. When Adam and Eve sinned, every dimension of their lives was affected. Their posterity has been affected in the same ways. We all manifest our sin nature in various ways. One of them is homosexuality.

So, why does God permit people to be gay? I could answer the question easily if all gay people chose to be so. God chooses to honor the free will he gives us; consequently, our misused freedom is not his fault but ours. However, the majority of gay people say that they did not choose to be homosexual. Their sexual identity may be a product of their genetics or circumstances but, either way, it's not their fault.

How can God be fair and permit them to struggle with this problem?

Let's note this fact: Every word used in the Old or New Testament to describe homosexuals refers to action: "have sex with them" (Genesis 19:5); "lie with a man" (Leviticus 18:22 ESV); "if a man lies with a male" (Leviticus 20:13 ESV); "shameless acts" (Romans 1:27 ESV); "men who practice homosexuality" (1 Corinthians 6:9; 1 Timothy 1:10 ESV). In every case, the Hebrew or Greek words refer to the actions involved, not the persons themselves.

As a result, it seems to me that the Bible does not condemn a person for being tempted by homosexual activity. However, it forbids the person to act on those inclinations since such actions are harmful to the person and others. The Bible does not condemn me for noticing a beautiful woman, only for acting on that attraction. It does not condemn you for being angry with people who have hurt you, only for acting on that anger by hurting them. It's not wrong to want popularity or wealth, but it is wrong to act sinfully to achieve those goals.

God does not make people gay. He permits some to be gay by nature or nurture as a result of this fallen world, just as he permits all of us to experience a sin nature as a result of the Fall. He does not reject us for being disposed toward sin, but he condemns the sin that comes from acting on that disposition.

So, given the biblical truths on this issue, how can Christians hold to God's word in a way that is also in keeping with God's heart?

Sexual sin and God's grace

Homosexual people deserve to be treated with dignity and respect. If they act on their orientation, they behave in ways that are unbiblical and often harmful to themselves and others. But so do those who practice slander, gossip, heterosexual lust, or egotistical pride. Any action or attitude that makes it harder for people to live a life God can bless is the opposite of the grace and unconditional love of Christ.

At the same time, while we must offer the dignity and respect of Christian grace to all persons, we cannot truly love them while endorsing that which is unbiblical in their lives.

As the body of Christ, we should want nothing more than to be able to tell people who sincerely struggle with the feeling that they are attracted to someone of the same gender that it's acceptable to embrace those emotions, to live the life that feels most right to them. But we cannot.

What we can and must do is recognize that every person is more than their sexual orientation and treat them accordingly. None of us want to be known or identified by one aspect of our lives, but, far too often, the church has been guilty of approaching those living in sexual sin of any kind as if their orientation or lusts equaled the sum total of who they are.

Think of how strongly you would react to a person who judged you in the same way. Perhaps then you can begin to understand why so many in our culture have ignored or denounced the Christian message in this area.

Fortunately, it doesn't have to be this way. Hope and grace exist for those struggling with sexual sins, just as hope and grace exist for sinners of every sort. The church has been given the tremendous responsibility and privilege of sharing this good news with those who so desperately need to hear it.

After including homosexuality in his list of sins (1 Corinthians 6:9), Paul next told the Corinthians: "And that is what some of you were.`But you were washed,`you were sanctified,`you were justified`in the name of the Lord Jesus Christ and by the Spirit of our God" (v. 11).

I have known homosexual men and women who were transformed by God's power so fully that they were freed of their homosexual desires. Some now live in an asexual orientation, while many experience heterosexual desires that can be satisfied within a biblical marriage covenant. What God did for the Corinthians, he can do for us today.

As Christians tasked with holding to God's truth regardless of what the culture around us may believe, it is vital that we understand not only what the Bible says on the subject of sexual sin but also the proper way to help others accept that understanding as well. Speaking the truth in love means far more than just not speaking it in hate. It requires living the truth out in our lives and in our relationships with other people in a way that makes them consider an argument they might prefer not to believe.

We can and should be confident that God's truth on the subject of sexual sin is correct and relevant, but those who reject biblical authority will not be convinced by biblical arguments until they are first convinced by the lives of those who believe the Bible.

As we'll see in the next chapter, the same is largely true for the issue of gender identity.

4

THE SUBJECTIVITY OF GENDER IDENTITY: HOW TRANSGENDERISM CONFUSES THE CULTURE

In the last chapter, we examined some of the ways that our nation's marginalization of objective truth and the authority of God's word impacted the way our culture views sexual sins. The same elements have also profoundly impacted the way that many view gender norms and the degree to which it is possible to speak of gender objectively.

The conflict over how gender identity should be understood plays out mostly in discussions over bathrooms and pronouns, but the truth is that the real issues are of a more fundamental nature. As we will see, God's word speaks directly to these issues, calling us to obey his truth and persuade our culture to do the same.

What is "transgender"?

Let's begin with definitions. The American Psychological Association (APA) defines "transgender" as "an umbrella term for persons whose gender identity, gender expression or behavior does not conform to that typically associated with the sex to which they were assigned at birth." "Gender identity" is "a person's internal sense of being male, female or something else."

"Gender expression" is "the way a person communicates gender identity through behavior, clothing, hairstyles, voice or body characteristics."[27] "Gender dysphoria" is a general term for "strong, persistent feelings of identification with another gender and discomfort with one's own assigned gender and sex; in order to qualify for a diagnosis of gender dysphoria, these feelings must cause significant distress or impairment."[28]

The APA explains that "sex" is assigned at birth, referring to one's biological status as either male or female. "Gender refers to the socially constructed roles, behaviors, activities, and attributes that a given society considers appropriate for boys and men or girls and women."

A "transgender" person, then, is someone who identifies with a different gender than their sex—a male who identifies as a female (MTF, or "male to female"), or a female who identifies as a male (FTM, or "female to male").

Transgender people may or may not seek hormonal and/or sex reassignment surgery to conform their bodies to their gender identities. Those who undergo such medical procedures are called "transsexual," as they have transitioned physically from one sex to another. A person born as a male becomes recognizably female, and vice versa.

Why are some people transgender?

The APA states that "there is no single explanation for why some people are transgender." It cites experts who believe that "biological factors such as genetic influences and prenatal hormone levels, early experiences, and experiences later in adolescence or adulthood may all contribute to the development of transgender identities."

Researchers have also discovered physical factors that may contribute to transgender experience. For instance, recent studies found that the brains of FTM transgender subjects contained white matter in regions resembling a male brain. In other words, these brains were "masculinized." Similarly, the brains of MTF transgender subjects were found to be "not completely masculinized and not completely feminized."[29]

Another study employed androstadienone, an odorous steroid known to cause a different response in the hypothalamus of women versus men. Using functional MRI, investigators discovered that transgender boys and girls responded to the odor much like peers of their identified gender. In other words, MTF persons responded instinctively like females; FTM persons responded instinctively like males.[30] A similar study using functional MRI to measure verbal fluency suggested "a biological basis for both transgender groups performing in-between the two sexes."[31]

Other studies have posited a variety of physical factors for gender dysphoria, including genetic components,[32] regional gray matter variation in the brain,[33] and galanin neurons in the hypothalamus.[34] A study of transsexuality among twins concluded that "their identity was much more influenced by their genetics than by their rearing."[35]

However, studies on neuroplasticity show that some brain structures can be modified by circumstances such as parenting and repeated activities.[36] In other words, it is entirely plausible that possible transgender brain factors may be the result of life circumstances rather than inherent conditions. The nature versus nurture argument is relevant to this issue as to so many others.

In addition, the (possible) presence of biological factors does not necessarily warrant acceptance of behavior associated with these factors. A person's biological conditions and aptitudes are not the only factors in determining appropriate moral and practical standards.

For example, as we discussed in the last chapter, even if a so-called "gay gene" were to be discovered, we would still debate the morality of homosexual activity and marriage in light of biblical truth. Some feel the same way with regard to transgender people. We are fallen people living in a fallen world.

In addition, some identify their gender as falling outside the constructs of "male" or "female" and are referred to as "genderqueer."

They may prefer pronouns such as "zie" instead of "he" or "she."

Other categories of transgender people include "intersex," "androgynous," "multigendered," "gender nonconforming," "third gender," and "two-spirit people." Reflecting the complexity of this issue, there are now more than fifty gender options on Facebook.

Ultimately, it's clear that in many circumstances pinpointing the reason why a transgender person does not identify with their biological sex is far more complicated than many would want to believe. For our culture, that's often enough to validate the argument that people should be free to identify as whatever gender feels most right to them. However, for those who still believe in the objective truth and relevance of God's word, that's not where the conversation ends.

A biblical response

It seems clear that people can experience gender dysphoria in a number of ways and for a number of reasons. How do we reconcile this fact with Scripture?

To begin, God's word is clear that he "created mankind in his own image, in the image of God he created them; male and female he created them" (Genesis 1:27; affirmed by Jesus in Matthew 19:4). Of course, many in the transgender movement would agree with that statement, claiming that what they reject is the belief that they must identify with their biological, God-given sex.

In response, we can point out that the Bible does not differentiate between gender and sex. Moreover, if forced to parse the two, this passage in Genesis clearly speaks more to gender than sex, as it states that God made both male and female in his image. As God cannot be biologically male and biologically female, what he had in mind with the creation of two genders must be about a deeper identity.

We'll discuss the best way to understand those issues of identity next, but it's important to note that God clearly purposed a difference between the genders and wove that distinction into the creation of male and female. And while there is a range of ways in which individuals can manifest the female and male characteristics of God, boundaries have been established by the Lord. He did not intend to let us decide with which gender we want to identify. That choice has already been made.

Second, Scripture says far less about how we are meant to live out our gender identity than is often perceived. There are not really any examples of character qualities (bravery, compassion, intelligence, etc.) that the Bible prescribes to male or female. That truth is important for the present discussion as many times the reason a person feels as though they were born into the wrong body is that they do not fit the stereotypes for their biological sex.[37]

There are a variety of ways, however, that a person can fulfill their God-given calling in this life, even within the same field. The diversity of personalities one finds among pastors, for example, is often directly related to the needs of the church that each pastor leads. In the classroom, there is far from one personality that equips a person to teach students. To limit the expression of a person's purpose in life to a preset list of characteristics or qualities is to place boundaries that God did not necessarily intend.

And the same basic principles apply to interests as well. There is nothing fundamentally wrong with a man who likes ballet or a woman who likes to hunt.

If a person feels as though they do not fit the gender norms associated with their biological sex, it's most likely because those associations are problematic. When we attempt to define masculinity and femininity in ways that God does not, then we are contributing to the problem.

Lastly, the Bible calls us to express our created sexual identity: "A woman must not wear men's clothing, nor a man wear women's clothing, for the` Lord` your God detests anyone who does this"

(Deuteronomy 22:5). The Lord cares far less about what a person wears than he does what that choice represents about their heart and intentions. A woman who wears a suit to a meeting or in a place of business, for example, is not in violation of this passage. Rather, God condemns the attempt to portray oneself as fundamentally different than who he created you to be.

The heavenly Father created each of his children for a unique and specific purpose, and gender plays an important part in that purpose. Because he knows that any attempts to live outside of his will make it exponentially more difficult to find the kind of peace, joy, and abundant life that is only found by walking with him, embracing your God-given gender is of paramount importance.

We will never find our place in God's kingdom if we can't accept who God made us to be. That truth extends far beyond issues of gender, but its relevance to the present conversation cannot be overstated.

How Christians often address these issues

In light of these principles, Christians typically lean toward one of three very different approaches to the question of transgender rights.

One: View transgender people as God's creation, worthy of full inclusion and support.

Jesus was especially compassionate toward those whom society marginalized. He accepted and defended children (Matthew 18:10) and would want us to do the same. In this view, a person who deals with gender dysphoria should be affirmed and protected as part of "the least of these" (Matthew 25:45).

This is the view taken by many who argue for transgender rights. It is also the view that most closely aligns with the general trajectory of the culture. As a result, many argue that it offers a middle ground to help Christians remain relevant without violating biblical principles (so long as the issue is interpreted primarily through the lens of Jesus' compassion to the socially marginalized). It's easy to see why many well-meaning Christians would be attracted to this approach.

However, it seems to conflict with the biblical statements cited above. Additionally, it ignores the fact that Jesus' compassion toward the socially marginalized did not include a blanket acceptance of their lifestyles. God's heart breaks for the person who genuinely feels as though they were born in the wrong body or, for any number of reasons, are tempted to try and find belonging and purpose by identifying with a gender other than their biological sex. He understands their pain in a way that only a parent can.

Yet his compassion for their circumstances does not change the reality of their situation. His word makes clear that the kind of acceptance and identity for which so many in the transgender community long is only to be found in him and by embracing his will for their lives. As Christians, if we offer solutions that conflict with God's, then we really aren't helping, even if it seems that we are.

Two: Refuse to address this issue.

Since the Bible seems clearly to state that God made us "male and female" (Genesis 1:27), some see the concept of "gender dysphoria" as illegitimate. In their view, such people should either decide to live according to their biological gender or medically change their gender.

While this view can be construed to align with the biblical statements cited above, it does not consider medical evidence indicating that unchosen physiological factors may contribute to at least some transgender experiences. Moreover, it completely ignores the basic fact that changing a person's biological sex to match their preferred gender means attempting to change God's divinely ordained will for their lives.

Ultimately, there are few within the Christian or the secular community that would be pleased with this solution. As such, it is not one that a well-meaning disciple of Christ should consider.

Three: Find a redemptive way to minister to everyone.

While transgender advocates and critics would both claim their position is best for all involved, neither side agrees with the other. I am advocating a third approach.

Jesus clearly affirmed that God made us "male and female" (Matthew 19:4). However, he also called us to minister to all people, regardless of their physical, emotional, psychological, or social challenges. He was famous for touching lepers, welcoming prostitutes, and befriending social outcasts. He was able to be compassionate without compromising biblical truth, and he wants us to follow his example.

The best way forward

In this spirit, I suggest the following principles.

One: Protect the vast majority of people who are not transgender or intersex and do not want people who display opposite-sex genitalia to share bathrooms, locker rooms, or showers with them or their children.

Two: Seek ways to minister to those with gender dysphoria in the context of God's best for their lives.

I view gender dysphoria as another evidence of the Fall and its consequences in our world. Few parents would want their children to live as transgender or believe that this is the best, most fulfilling life they can have. So, share the gospel with those who have not trusted Christ as their Savior. Offer community in Christ and help for physical and/or psychological challenges. In short, seek to help transgender people live according to their biological gender.

At the same time, we must understand that those who deal with gender dysphoria are not worse or better than anyone else. They are absolutely not to be bullied or otherwise harmed. A 2013 study found that nearly 70 percent of transgender people had experienced significant discrimination when trying to use the restroom.[38] But God loves them as much as he loves anyone else, including you and me. We are all broken people who live in a broken world.

Three: Seek practical solutions that are fair to all.

If the law eventually dictates that transgender people must be provided bathrooms, locker rooms, and showers in keeping with their gender identity, there are ways to provide such facilities without discriminating against the vast majority of the population.

In defending his administration's directive regarding transgender legislation, President Obama pointed to "our obligation as a society to make sure that everybody is treated fairly, and our kids are all loved, and that they're protected and that their dignity is affirmed."[39] He was speaking of transgender students, but his sentiment surely applies to the other fifty million students in America today. How can we protect them while providing legally required facilities for transgender students?

1. Create and/or designate single-use bathrooms, showers, and locker rooms. Many movie theaters are now being built with such facilities. Rather than Men's and Ladies' rooms, they offer a row of single-use bathrooms. Men's bathrooms could be configured to remove urinals and provide only privacy stalls. Many schools have such facilities for their teachers; these could be configured for transgender use as well.

2. Determine which athletic programs can be opened to transgender students without compromising the integrity of the sport and its participants. Where there are clear and unfair advantages for transgender students, their participation should not be allowed. One student's gender identity should not be permitted to compromise an entire athletic program for the rest of the student body.

3. Engage the entire community in these decisions before they are made. The last thing supporters on either side of the aisle need is to feel as though their voice on this subject doesn't matter. Discussing these issues in a way that gives room for each side to have a say in the final decision could go a long way toward helping to bring about solutions that both sides can accept, even if they aren't solutions that both sides would completely endorse.

As Christians ministering to a culture that often thinks very differently than we do on issues like those surrounding gender dysphoria, it's necessary to understand that working to make the lives better of those who do not adhere to biblical standards does not lessen the truth of God's word. I remain convinced that God's best is for people not to live with gender dysphoria. For this reason, I advocate for ministry to them intended to help them live within biblical guidelines and our Father's intention for his children. But, at the same time, we can't minister to them unless we're willing to listen to them.

Separate bathrooms, open dialogue, and taking their concerns seriously are important first steps to earning the right to share God's truth on this very personal subject.

Conclusion

The issue of transgender rights will continue to escalate in our culture since it pits two narratives that have been in conflict for years.

On one side is the insistence on tolerance that characterizes postmodern relativism. In a society with no objective truths, every truth can be tolerated unless it is deemed intolerant. This approach extends to gender identity just as it does to abortion rights, same-sex marriage, euthanasia, and a host of other moral challenges.

On the other side is the conviction that God made us and has a perfect will for our lives (Romans 12:1–2). This conviction entails a commitment to biblical truth as unchanging and authoritative, two values our postmodern culture rejects.

Those of us who believe that the Bible is still the truth of God will face escalating pressure to compromise our convictions or be seen as intolerant. Let us continue to speak the truth in love (Ephesians 4:15), claiming God's promise that his word "will accomplish what I desire and achieve the purpose for which I sent it" (Isaiah 55:11).

In engaging the culture, as in all kingdom service, our Lord measures success by obedience, and such obedience requires respecting biblical truth as well as those with whom we share it. That's how Jesus did it, and it's what our society needs from his followers today.

SECTION TWO

How do
Americans
relate to
each other?

INTRODUCTION

In the first section, we examined the degree to which Americans respect God's truth, with results that were less than encouraging. Will the same prove true with regard to our respect for each other?

Let's begin with some definitions.

While there is a clear biblical distinction between those who have been adopted into the family of God and those who have not, God's affection is equal for both groups.[40] Jesus is clear that God loved the entire world enough to send Christ to die for our sins (John 3:16), a point that Paul expands upon in his letter to the Romans (Romans 5:6–11).

Peter plainly states that God's desire is for no one to perish but all to become his children through repentance and faith in him (2 Peter 3:9). And the Lord repeatedly warned both his people and the nations at large that they would be judged for the way that they treated each other, demonstrating his care and concern even for those who cared nothing for him.

In the end, while God does give special attention to how people treat his children and the least of these, his word clearly teaches that he loves everyone enough to hold us accountable for how we treat one another, regardless of an individual's standing before him.

In this section, we will take a closer look at how America is treating the unborn, the impoverished, and those of different races. These chapters will help us determine where our society stands in God's eyes on this significant subject.

As you read, do so with the understanding that this is likely the area where God's people can make the greatest impact on our country and on the kingdom. However, we can only make such an impact if we remember that right belief, while vitally important, is only relevant to the lost around us when accompanied by right action. If our respect for God's truth is not coupled with a respect for one another, then we will not be his salt and light today (Matthew 5:13–16).

5

KILLING THE UNBORN: WHY ABORTION IS A CHOICE NONE SHOULD MAKE

The first test for how well Americans respect one another is how we treat children. Scripture is abundantly clear that the Father's concern for little ones is absolute and unconditional. Jesus exemplified such love in the way that he received them, while simultaneously explaining that all who welcome children welcome him as well.

Our Lord then warned that the consequences were dire for those who caused them to stumble or sin (Matthew 18:2–6, Mark 10:13–16). The Lord, who loves all life and holds it sacred, repeatedly warns in his word that those who take life will face his wrath.

So, how is our nation caring for children?

We'll start with the youngest by examining our culture's approach to the unborn.

Abortion: The ethical crisis of our day

In 2015, 35,485 people died on American roadways. Every eighteen days, that number of abortions were performed in the US. That year, doctors conducted 638,169 abortions in America, exceeding the total number killed in the Civil War.

Since the US Supreme Court's *Roe v. Wade* decision legalized abortion in January of 1973, more than sixty-one million abortions have been performed in America. This is a number larger than the combined populations of Kentucky, Oregon, Oklahoma, Connecticut, Iowa, Mississippi, Arkansas, Kansas, Utah, Nevada, New Mexico, West Virginia, Nebraska, Idaho, Maine, New Hampshire, Hawaii, Rhode Island, Montana, Delaware, South Dakota, Alaska, North Dakota, Vermont, and Wyoming. Depending on the year, an abortion occurs for every three or four live births in our country.

Why do so many people in America believe that a mother should have the right to choose direct abortion?

Roe v. Wade overturned state laws limiting a woman's right to abortion.[41] The Court's decision was largely based on the argument that the Constitution nowhere defines a fetus as a person or protects the rights of the unborn.

Rather, the Court determined that an unborn baby possesses only "potential life" and is not yet a "human being" or "person." It argued that every constitutional reference to "person" relates to those already born. The Fourteenth Amendment guarantees protections and rights to individuals, but the Court ruled that the amendment does not include the unborn.

The Court further determined that a woman's "right to privacy" extends to her ability to make her own choices regarding her health and body. Just as she has the right to choose to become pregnant, she has the right to end that pregnancy. The Court suggested several specific reasons why she might choose abortion:

- "Specific and direct harm" may come to her.
- "Maternity, or additional offspring, may force upon the woman a distressful life and future."
- "Psychological harm may be imminent."
- "Mental and physical health may be taxed by child care."
- Problems may occur associated with bearing unwanted children.
- "The additional difficulties and continuing stigma of unwed motherhood" should be considered.[42]

Since 1973, four positions have been taken in the abortion debate:

- There should be no right to an abortion, even to save the life of the mother. This has been the Catholic Church's usual position.

- Therapeutic abortions can be performed to save the mother's life.

- Extreme-case abortions can be permitted in cases of rape, incest, or severe deformation of the fetus. (Most pro-life advocates would accept therapeutic and extreme case abortions.)

- Abortion should be available to any woman who chooses it. This is the typical pro-choice position.

Arguments for and against abortion

When debating the issue of abortion, pro-choice advocates typically make five basic claims:

First, pro-choice proponents argue that a fetus is not legally a "person."

They agree with the Supreme Court's finding that the Constitution nowhere grants legal standing to a preborn life. Only 40 to 50 percent of fetuses survive to become persons in the full sense. A fetus belongs to the mother until it attains personhood and is morally subject to any action she wishes to take with it.

Pro-life advocates counter that a fetus is a human life and should be granted the full protection of the law. The fetus carries its parents' genetic code and is a distinct person. It does not yet possess self-consciousness, reasoning ability, or moral awareness (the usual descriptions of a "person")—but neither do newborns or young children. As this is the central issue of the debate, we'll say more about it in a moment.

Second, abortion must be protected as an alternative for women who are the victims of rape or incest.

While this number is admittedly small in the US (approximately 1 percent of all abortions), it is growing in many countries around the world. As many as one in three women may become the victim of such an attack. Society must spare them the further trauma of pregnancy and childbirth, it is claimed.

Most pro-life advocates are willing to permit abortion in cases of rape and incest or to protect the life of the mother. While not all agree, such cases typically account for only 1 to 4 percent of abortions performed so limiting abortion to these conditions would still prevent the vast majority of abortions occurring in America.

Third, no unwanted children should be brought into the world.

If a woman does not wish to bear a child, she clearly will not be an appropriate or effective mother if the child is born. Given the population explosion occurring in many countries, abortion is a necessary option for women who do not want children. The woman is more closely involved with the fetus than any other individual and is the best person to determine whether or not this child is wanted and will receive proper care.

Pro-life advocates agree that all children should be wanted, so they argue strongly for adoption as an alternative to abortion. They also assert that an unwanted child would rather live than die, making this perhaps the weakest pro-choice argument in favor of abortion. After all, by pro-choice logic, it would be possible to argue for infanticide and all forms of euthanasia as well.[43]

Fourth, the state has no right to legislate our personal moral decisions.

While the government should be free to impose legislation on moral questions when this legislation expresses the clear, moral consensus of the community and when it prevents conduct that obviously threatens the public welfare, Americans are divided on the morality of abortion. It is hard to see how aborting a fetus threatens the rest of the community.

Moreover, since there is no constitutional standard for when life begins, decisions made regarding a fetus are a matter for individual morality. And so abortion should not be subject to governmental control. It is better to allow a mother to make this decision than to legislate it through governmental action. Many who personally consider abortion to be wrong are persuaded by this argument and thus support the pro-choice position.

Pro-life supporters do not see abortion legislation as an intrusion into areas of private morality. Protecting the rights of the individual is the state's first responsibility. No moral state can overlook murder, whatever the personal opinions of those who commit it. The state is especially obligated to protect the rights of those who cannot defend themselves.

But what of the claim that legislation must always reflect the clear will of the majority and protect the public welfare? The collective will of the culture must never supersede what is right and wrong. For instance, heroin is so popular that as many as 4.2 million Americans say they've used it at least once. Nonetheless, we ban it because its harmful effects are clear to medical science. The effects of abortion on a fetus are obviously even more disastrous to the fetus. And just because society is unclear as to when life begins does not mean that the question is unknowable. The very fact that the Supreme Court's interpretation leaves open the possibility that a fetus is a person means the law should protect it so as to guard against the possibility of sanctioning murder.

If more of the public understood the physical and ethical issues involved in abortion, a large majority would consider abortion to be a threat to public welfare. Abortion threatens the entire community in three ways:

1. It ends the lives of millions, on a level exceeding all wars and disasters combined.

2. It encourages sexual promiscuity.

3. It permits women to make a choice that will plague many of them with guilt for years to come.

And so, abortion meets the standard for legislative relevance and must be addressed and limited or abolished by the state.

Fifth, the rights and concerns of the mother must take precedence over those of the fetus.

Even if we grant fetuses limited rights, they must not supersede the rights of mothers, as the latter are clearly persons under the Constitution. If we allow abortion to protect her physical life, we should do so to protect her emotional health or quality of life as well.

This was one of the Court's most significant arguments, as it sought to protect the mother's mental and physical health. Many pro-choice advocates are especially persuaded by this argument and view the abortion debate within the context of a woman's right to control her own life.

However, the argument can (and should) also be made that, except in matters of mortal danger, there are no grounds for having to choose between the health of the mother and the child. As the rights of a mother are no more important than those of her newborn infant, so they are no more important than those of her preborn child. The stress, guilt, and long-term mental anguish reported by many who abort their children must be considered.

Killing the fetus for the sake of the mother's health is like remedying paranoia by killing all the imagined persecutors. For these reasons, pro-life advocates argue that a moral state must limit or prevent abortion.

Why the unborn child is worth protecting

The pro-life position outlined above only makes sense, however, if the unborn child is worth protecting. If life does not begin until the fetus is viable or the child is born, one can argue that the "right to life" does not extend to the preborn and abortion should be considered both legal and moral. But if life begins prior to that point, there can be no moral justification for abortion since this action kills an innocent person.

So, when does life begin? There are essentially three answers to the question.

1. "Functionalism" states that the fetus is a "person" when it can act personally as a moral, intellectual, and spiritual agent. (Note that, by this definition, some question whether a newborn infant would be considered a "person.")

2. "Actualism" is the position that a fetus is a person if it possesses the potential for developing self-conscious, personal life. This definition would permit abortion when the fetus clearly does not possess the capacity for functional life.

3. "Essentialism" argues that the fetus is a person from conception, whatever its health or potential. It is an individual in the earliest stages of development and deserves all the protections afforded to other persons by our society.

So, can we determine when life begins? Our answer depends on the definition of "life."

A pro-choice advocate recognizes that the fetus is alive in the sense that it is a biological entity. But so is every other part of a woman's body. Some consider the fetus to be a "growth" and liken it to a tumor or other unwanted tissue. Biology alone is not enough to settle the issue.

What about capacity? Many ethicists define a "person" as someone able to respond to stimuli, interact with others, and make individual decisions. A fetus meets the first two standards from almost the moment of its conception and clearly cannot fulfill the third only because it is enclosed in its mother's body. Would a newborn baby fulfill these three conditions?

What about individuality? If we view a fetus as a "growth" within the mother's body, it would be easier to sanction her choice to remove that growth if she wishes. But a fetus is distinct from its mother from the moment of its conception. It is alive—it reacts to stimuli and can produce its own cells and develop them into a specific pattern of maturity. It is human, completely distinguishable from all other living organisms, possessing all forty-six human chromosomes, able to develop only into a human being. And it is complete—nothing new will be added except the growth and development of what exists from the moment of conception.

It is a scientific fact that every abortion performed in the United States is performed on a being so fully formed that its heart is beating and its brain activity can be measured on an EEG machine. At twelve weeks, the unborn baby is only about two inches long, yet every organ of the human body is clearly in place.

And note that you did not come from a fetus—you were a fetus. A "fetus" is simply a human life in the womb. It becomes a "baby" outside the womb. But it is the same physical entity in either place.

For these reasons, pro-life advocates believe that the US Supreme Court was wrong in deciding that a fetus is not a person entitled to the full protections of the law. Apart from spiritual or moral concerns, it is a simple fact of biology that the fetus possesses every attribute of human life we find in a newborn infant, with the exception of independent physical viability. Left unharmed, it will soon develop this capacity as well. If a life must be independently viable to be viewed as a person, a young child might well fail this standard, as would those of any age facing severe physical challenges.

However, regardless of whether an individual believes that the aforementioned characteristics mean that a fetus constitutes a person, it is clear that the unborn are living creatures. Would those who are unwilling to grant them equal rights with a child who has been born see the preborn as deserving the basic protections offered to animals and livestock? The question might sound strange, but many of the methods by which abortions are provided would seem to answer in the negative.

What follows in the next section will be difficult to read. We hesitated to include it and have done our best to limit its graphic nature where possible, but the information and its implications are too important to overlook.

Methods of abortion

Abortions in the US are performed in the following ways, depending on the gestation period.

First trimester

A baby's heart begins beating at eighteen days after conception. By the fourth week, the baby's brain and spinal cord are developing. In the fifth week, legs begin to form; by the tenth week, the baby is developing distinct arms and legs, fingers and toes, fingernails, and genitals.[44]

During this period of development, the following methods are used to abort the baby.

- Methotrexate and Misoprostol (MTX): Methotrexate is given to the mother orally or by injection. Antibiotics are also given to prevent infection. Three to seven days later, Misoprostol tablets are given orally or inserted vaginally. The procedure usually triggers contractions and expels the baby, a process that may take a few hours or as long as a few days.

- Mifepristone and Misoprostol (RU-486): Mifepristone is given orally to the mother. It blocks the production of progesterone needed for the baby to develop. Misoprostol is taken six to forty-eight hours later. It causes cramping and bleeding to empty the uterus and end the pregnancy. Bleeding can continue for several weeks.

- Aspiration: A catheter is inserted into the mother's uterus to suction out the preborn baby. The doctor then uses tools to scrape the lining of the uterus to remove any remaining parts. The fetus will either be torn apart by this procedure, or it will be suctioned into the tube and then into a gauze bag that traps the fetal structure. Abortion providers have testified that the fetus' heart can still be beating throughout the procedure.[45]

Second trimester

During the second trimester, the baby's fingers and toes become well-defined; eyelids, eyebrows, eyelashes, nails, and hair are formed; and teeth and bones become denser. The baby can suck his or her thumb, yawn, stretch, and make faces. By the sixth month, the baby can respond to sounds. Fingerprints and toe prints are visible. The eyelids begin to part and the eyes to open.[46]

Medication-based abortions are not an option at this point in the baby's development. The following procedures are used:

- Dilation and Cuterrage (D & C): The cervix is dilated, and a long, spoon-shaped instrument called a curette is used to scrape the lining of the uterus to remove it from the mother's body. A cannula may also be used to suction any remaining uterine contents.

- Dilation and Evacuation (D & E): Similar to D & C, except that forceps are used to dismember the baby's body before it is removed. The skull has often hardened to bone by this time and must be compressed or crushed to facilitate removal.

- Salt poisoning: A solution of concentrated salt is inserted into the amniotic fluid. The baby breathes in, swallowing the salt, and is poisoned. The chemical solution also causes burning and deterioration of the baby's skin. The child dies after about an hour.

Third trimester

During the last trimester of an unborn child's life, the following abortion procedures are used:

- Induction abortion: The doctor injects digoxin or potassium chloride into the baby, targeting its heart, torso, or head. The drug causes a fatal cardiac arrest. A few days later, the mother delivers the dead baby.

- Dilation and Extraction ("partial-birth abortion"): The mother is prematurely dilated, then the baby is vaginally delivered until the entire body except for the head is out of the body. The doctor then punctures the back of the head and suctions out the brain or crushes the skull, then completes the delivery of the now-deceased baby.

Abortion and public consensus

These methods are coming under increasing scrutiny for a variety of reasons.

One is that scientific advances make it increasingly clear that a "fetus" is a baby. As one mother notes, "When you're seeing a baby sucking its thumb at 18 weeks, smiling, clapping," it becomes "harder to square the idea that that 20-week old, that unborn baby or fetus, is discardable."[47]

Ultrasounds show the baby's physical development with remarkable clarity. Studies demonstrate that the fetus feels pain early in his or her development. Surgeons can operate on fetuses in the womb, showing the illogic of valuing them as less than human.

A second factor is opposition to the death penalty and to inhumane treatment of animals. By logic, such opposition should extend to the practice of abortion.

Current methods of capital punishment include hanging, shooting, lethal injection, electrocution, gas inhalation, and beheading (used only in Saudi Arabia).[48] No civilized nation would allow a convicted criminal to be executed using methods such as those that are employed in nonmedical legal abortions.

Animals cannot be legally killed for food unless they are first stunned so that they are unconscious and feel no pain.[49] Even this provision is not made for babies prior to being aborted. As both sides continue to debate the legality of Roe v Wade, can we not at least agree that our unborn children deserve the same protections as livestock?

The Bible and abortion

All of the previous statements are based on moral claims and legal arguments. They are intended to persuade society regardless of a person's religious persuasion.

As a result, they demonstrate that it is not possible to claim ignorance or innocence on the topic of abortion simply because people do not believe in the Christian God. All Americans are fully capable of making the morally correct choice on this issue, and all will be held accountable for that choice as a result.

But many in our culture also want to know what the Bible says on this crucial subject.[50] Is Scripture clear on the personhood of a fetus or the morality of abortion? As we will see, while the term *abortion* appears nowhere in the Bible, God's word is far from silent on the topic.

Silent on the issue?

No one in the Bible is ever described as having an abortion, encouraging one, or even dealing with one. But this does not mean that Scripture is silent on the issue. The word *trinity* nowhere appears in God's word. Nor does *marijuana* or *cocaine*. But these are all relevant issues for which Scripture offers clear guidance.

The Bible does not address abortion specifically because this was not an issue in question for the Jewish and early Christian communities. *The Sentences of Pseudo-Phocylides*, the *Mishnah*, the *Didache*, and the *Epistle of Barnabas* were written shortly before Christ or within the first century of the Christian era. Each expresses their faith community's clear prohibition of abortion.

Important biblical passages

While the Bible does not use the word *abortion*, it contains a number of texts that relate directly to the beginning of life and the value of all persons. Let's look briefly at the most pertinent passages.

First, pro-choice scholars often cite this statement in Exodus to argue that Scripture values the life of the mother differently than the life of her child: "When people who are fighting injure a pregnant woman so that there is a miscarriage, and yet no further harm follows, the one responsible shall be fined what the woman's husband demands, paying as much as the judges determine. If any harm follows, then you shall give life for life, eye for eye, tooth for tooth, hand for hand, foot for foot, burn for burn, wound for wound, stripe for stripe" (Exodus 21:22–25, NRSV).

However, the New International Version translates the text as "she gives birth prematurely but there is no serious injury." The New Living Translation similarly states, "They accidentally strike a pregnant woman so she gives birth prematurely. If no further harm results . . . ." The English Standard Version renders the phrase "so that her children come out, but there is no harm."

Verse 23 settles the issue: "But if there is serious injury . . . ." (NIV), implying that no serious injury occurred in verse 22. In other words, both the mother and her child survived the attack and were healthy. And so, this passage does not devalue the preborn life or speak specifically to the issue of abortion.

Second, some theorize that Genesis 2:7—"Then the Lord God formed a man from the dust of the ground and breathed into his nostrils the breath of life, and the man became a living being"—means that life does not begin until the fetus can breathe outside its mother's womb.

However, we know that a fetus is animate from the moment of its conception and that it breathes in the womb, exchanging amniotic fluid for air after birth. This text therefore applies only to Adam and his miraculous creation, not to humans conceived afterward.

Third, David thanked God because "you created my inmost being; you knit me together in my mother's womb. . . . Your eyes saw my unformed body; all the days ordained for me were written in your book before one of them came to be" (Psalm 139:13, 16). Pro-life theologians point to this declaration as proof that life is created by God and begins at conception.

Of course, those who do not accept the authority of Scripture will not be persuaded by this argument. And even some who do respect the Bible believe that David's statement is poetic symbolism rather than scientific description. They claim that he was simply stating that he is God's creation, without speaking specifically to the status of a fetus.

Fourth, the Lord told Jeremiah, "Before I formed you in the womb I knew you, before you were born I set you apart; I appointed you as a prophet to the nations" (Jeremiah 1:5). "Knew" translates the Hebrew *yada*, meaning "to understand, comprehend, know completely." God's plan for Jeremiah clearly began before he was born.

Fifth, when Mary visited Elizabeth, the latter told the former: "As soon as the sound of your greeting reached my ears, the baby in my womb leaped for joy" (Luke 1:44). Elizabeth's unborn child was a *brephos*, the Greek term for baby, embryo, fetus, newborn child, young child, or nursing child.

It is the same used of Jesus when the shepherds found "the baby, who was lying in the manger" (Luke 2:16). And of Timothy when Paul reminded him "how from *infancy* you have known the Holy Scriptures"

(2 Timothy 3:15, italics added). The Bible makes no distinction between the personhood of a human being, whether before or after its birth.

Sixth, the Bible consistently defends the rights of the innocent (cf. Exodus 23:7; Proverbs 6:16–19; 2 Kings 24:3–4). God clearly cares for the innocent and defenseless of the world. Children, whether before their birth or after, are among his most valued creations (cf. Matthew 18:1–5; 19:13–15).

What about rape and incest?

The Bible makes rape a capital offense (Deuteronomy 22:25–26). However, it has been established by numerous surveys over the years that rape and incest victims represent approximately 1 percent of the abortion cases annually recorded in America.

A decision to limit abortions to this exception would prevent the deaths of nearly all of the one million babies who are aborted each year. Only about 3 percent of the abortions performed each year in America relate to the health of the mother, and 3 percent relate to the health of the child. Ninety-three percent are elective.

At the same time, Americans should be conscious of the fact that rape and incest are far more common in some other countries and cultures. Rape, in particular, is a typical means of coercion and military control in some societies. There the percentage of abortions related to rape may be much higher than is the case in America.

This caveat stated, I'm not sure that even this decision is the moral choice. I must quickly admit that my status as an American white male makes it very difficult for me to identify with women around the world who have experienced such trauma as rape and incest. But it is hard for me to understand how the child produced by this terrible crime does not deserve to live.

Ethel Waters, the famous gospel singer, was the product of a rape. So was a student I taught at Southwestern Seminary, an evangelist with a global ministry today. I tread very lightly here but would, at the very least, suggest that this issue is far from the primary cause of abortion in America today.

A way forward?

Since participants in the abortion debate come from a variety of religious and personal worldviews, it seems implausible to find common ground by beginning with biblical teachings or religious convictions. As a result, I suggest the following nonreligious, constitutional strategy.

First, by allowing an exception for rape, incest, and the life of the mother, we remove the most obvious and emotional obstacle to the pro-life position. We can then focus on the 93 percent of abortions in America that are elective. It would also leave room to counsel mothers thinking about procuring an abortion for those reasons on a case-by-case basis.

Second, pro-life and pro-choice advocates should work together to fulfill President Bill Clinton's desire that abortion be "rare." [51] Surely even the most ardent pro-choice supporters would not object to a decrease in the number of abortions performed each year. Both sides could promote adoption and support abstinence and birth control education. Educating the public about the characteristics of a fetus has also been shown to help mothers choose to keep their unborn children.

Third, pro-life advocates must do all we can to care for both the unborn child as well as its mother and father. We must work to advocate adoption and to provide necessities for at-risk families. We need to be pro-life, not just pro-birth.

Conclusion

It is vital that Christians maintain our consistent commitment to biblical principles regarding the sanctity of life from the moment of conception. Abortion is a tragedy that affects the biological parents and extended family as well as the unborn child.

But it is also vital that we share these principles with grace, "speaking the truth in love" (Ephesians 4:15).

Would abortion be a moral choice when a family is extremely poor, with fourteen children and another on the way? That unborn child was John Wesley. What about a father who is ill and a mother with tuberculosis; their first child is blind, the second has died, the third is deaf, and the fourth has tuberculosis? Now she is pregnant again. Her son would be called Beethoven.

A white man rapes a thirteen-year-old black girl and she becomes pregnant. Her child is Ethel Waters. A teenage girl is pregnant, but her fiancée is not the father of the baby. Her baby is Jesus.

God loves every person from the moment of his or her conception. Do we?

6

CARING LITTLE FOR THE LEAST: HOW THE POOR, THE SICK, THE FOREIGN, AND THE JAILED REVEAL AMERICA'S TRUE FACE

In one of Jesus' final teachings to his disciples prior to his arrest and crucifixion, he told them a parable in which God separated the sheep from the goats in the final judgment (Matthew 25:21–46). His story was meant to emphasize the importance of demonstrating their faith through action.

Jesus stated that those who cared for the hungry, the thirsty, the foreigner, the naked, the sick, and the imprisoned—essentially those who were in dire need of care from others—ministered to him in the process. He also warned that those who ignored "the least of these" ignored him as well.[52] The first group he called sheep while the latter were goats.

His purpose in this story was not to advocate for works-based righteousness, but to emphasize that a faith that disregards those in need is foreign to the Lord. In so doing, he echoed the warnings delivered through the Old Testament prophets. Those who helped the least of these in Christ's parable did not know they were helping Jesus. Rather, their actions were the natural result of their relationship with him.

One of our greatest fears for the church in America today is that far too often our words and actions are more akin to the goats than the sheep. When we fail to see Christ in the face of the homeless, or when we look upon the foreigner with fear and contempt rather than empathy and respect, we find ourselves on the wrong side of God's divide. Again, this does not mean that our salvation hinges upon our treatment of others, as a personal relationship with Jesus is the only requirement to spend eternity with our heavenly Father.

But we must not take for granted that a faith without regard for those God loves is not liable to judgment.

So where does America stand on ministry to the "least of these"?

In the last chapter, we saw that our culture's accepted approach to the unborn could not be further removed from the heart of God. Is the same true for how we treat the poor, immigrants, or other groups with whom Jesus identified in his parable?

The least of these in America today

One of the most difficult aspects of gauging our nation's response to the least of these in our midst is that recognizing the problem is only the start. As James warns, if our response to the destitute is simply to wish them well but do nothing to actually meet their needs, it stands as evidence of a dead faith (James 2:15–17).

But how are we to go about meeting those needs? How can we help people in a way that truly improves their lives rather than simply delaying their hardships?

As we will see, there are no easy solutions to this matter. Moreover, the purpose of this chapter is not to advocate for any specific path as the only way forward. What is clear, however, is that we cannot simply ignore the least of these and think that our relationship with Christ will continue unhindered. Real action is necessary, be it on the national or local levels, and each of us has a role to play in this calling.

Fortunately, this topic has been taken up by Christians and non-Christians alike, often with the greatest emphasis coming from outside the church. And while one's favored solution to the following issues often falls along political party lines, the debate is healthy in so far as it can help us gain a greater understanding of the need and how to meet it.

To that end, we will begin our discussion with a look at the impoverished before moving on to issues like health care, immigration, and prison reform.

Poverty

According to PovertyUSA, more than forty million people in America live in poverty (defined by the US government as an income of less than $24,000 for a family of four).[53] This number comprises 16.3 percent of women and 13.8 percent of men.

More than 21 percent of all children live in poverty, as do more than 9 percent of seniors. More than 12 percent of all US households were food insecure in 2016.

The poverty rate for African Americans exceeds 21 percent; for Hispanics, 18 percent. For single mothers, the poverty rate exceeds 25 percent. For those with a disability, it exceeds 24 percent.[54]

Clearly, poverty is a crucial issue in America today and one in need of attention, but it is not alone. Immigrants, the sick, and the imprisoned are also among those with whom Jesus identified in the previously mentioned parable. How is our country doing in those areas?

Health Care

In 2017, 91.2 percent of Americans had health insurance of one form or another, with more than half the population receiving their coverage through an employment-based plan.[55] While health insurance is by no means the only, or even primary, measure of how a country deals with the sick, it can offer a helpful barometer of its priorities.

Debate dominates the news every time the government moves to pass legislation on this topic, typically resulting in more ideological arguments than substantive change. What this debate demonstrates, however, is that Americans are not willing to let their government ignore this issue. Just as Jesus cared for the sick, so must we.

Fortunately, we do not need to wait for the government before we offer help in this area. One of the most difficult parts of illness, especially one that creates a new normal for how a person lives going forward, is the sense of isolation it can breed. Providing a sense of community for the sick can play a crucial role in their rehabilitation. Taking meals to their families, sitting beside them in the waiting room, helping with their bills or other needs where possible, or any number of other, seemingly smaller tasks can make a greater difference than the government possibly could.

Immigration

Immigration is one of the most divisive issues in our country today, with sound, biblically based arguments espoused by people on both sides of the debate.

According to the Pew Research Center, 84 percent of Democrats and Democratic-leaning independents believe that immigrants "strengthen the country with their hard work and talents" while just 12 percent describe them as a burden.[56] Among Republicans and Republican-leaning independents, these statistics are 42 percent and 44 percent, respectively. Given that, as of 2016, more than 43 million people currently living in this country (or 13.5 percent of the population) were born somewhere else, this is clearly a discussion that will not go away soon.[57]

Roughly three-quarters of these immigrants are here legally while 45 percent are naturalized citizens. While Mexico is the most common country of origin for immigrants to our country, Mexican immigrants are far from the majority, accounting for roughly a quarter of those who sought to live in the US from afar. Additionally, refugees are often a key component of the immigration conversation, but they comprise a relatively small portion of the immigrant population, with slightly more coming from a Christian background (47 percent) than Muslim (43 percent) or other (10 percent).

Ultimately, whether one believes that immigrants are a blessing or a burden for our country, Jesus clearly cared a great deal about how we treat them on a personal level. If we reach the point where they become statistics before they are people, we have lost sight of God's heart on this critical subject. That does not necessarily mean open borders or turning a blind eye to our nation's laws, but we cannot afford to dehumanize anyone made in the image of God—which, to be clear, is everyone.

As Americans, we often face a similar problem with the last group that we will examine.

Prisoners

While it is tempting to see the imprisoned with whom Jesus identified in his parable as Christians who were arrested for their faith, it's important to remember that there was no one in prison for preaching the gospel when Jesus told this parable to the disciples. This situation changed quickly following Pentecost, but, for Jesus' initial audience, the implications of his message were far broader than many consider them today.

God absolutely cares for those who suffer as a result of their faith, but he also cares for those who suffer in general. Prisoners serving time as punishment for the laws they've broken are perhaps the easiest population in our society to ignore. Their suffering can seem justified because of their crimes, and, in many ways, it is. But God does not love them any less as a result, and Jesus clearly saw caring for them as a key part of our service to him.

As of December 2016, more than 6.6 million adults were incarcerated in our country. This number has been trending in an encouraging direction in recent years, declining every year since

2009. However, the US Department of Justice nonetheless stated that 2.6 percent of the American population over the age of eighteen was under some form of correctional supervision.[58]

Regardless of what a person did to earn his or her sentence, no one is ever beyond the reach of God's grace. Christ identified with the imprisoned because God loves them just as much as he did the disciples to whom Jesus was talking.

As a nation, there are few groups we are so quick to dehumanize as those in prison. This needs to change.

With this fact in mind, let's turn our attention to ways we can help take better care of the "least of these" around us so as to make a real difference in their lives.

How to help the "least of these"

See our service as an extension of God's love.

When Jesus began his public ministry, he was invited to speak in his hometown synagogue at Nazareth. He was handed the scroll of Isaiah but could have read from any of its sixty-six chapters.

Which would you expect him to select? Maybe Isaiah 9, with its promise of a "Wonderful Counselor, Almighty God, Everlasting Father, Prince of Peace"? Or Isaiah 53, with its incredibly precise prediction of his suffering and crucifixion?

Instead, here's what happened: "Unrolling it, he found the place where it is written: 'The Spirit of the Lord is on me, because he has anointed me to proclaim good news to the poor. He has sent me to proclaim freedom for the prisoners, and recovery of sight for the blind, to set the oppressed free, to proclaim the year of the Lord's favor'" (Luke 4:17–19, quoting Isaiah 61:1–2).

What happened next? "Then he rolled up the scroll, gave it back to the attendant and sat down. The eyes of everyone in the synagogue were fastened on him. He began by saying to them, 'Today this scripture is fulfilled in your hearing'" (Luke 4:20–21).

Why did Jesus know that his Father would bless a ministry that cared for the poor, the prisoners, the blind, and the oppressed? Because they had been at the center of his concern throughout human history:

- "He defends the cause of the fatherless and the widow, and loves the foreigner residing among you, giving them food and clothing" (Deuteronomy 10:18).

- "He will deliver the needy who cry out, the afflicted who have no one to help" (Psalm 72:12).

- "He will respond to the prayer of the destitute; he will not despise their plea" (Psalm 102:17).

- "The Lord secures justice for the poor and upholds the cause of the needy" (Psalm 140:12).

- "He upholds the cause of the oppressed and gives food to the hungry. The Lord sets prisoners free, the Lord gives sight to the blind, the Lord lifts up those who are bowed down, the Lord loves the righteous. The Lord watches over the foreigner and sustains the fatherless and the widow, but he frustrates the ways of the wicked" (Psalm 146:7–9).

- "You have been a refuge for the poor, a refuge for the needy in their distress, a shelter from the storm and a shade from the heat" (Isaiah 25:4).

What does God want us to do for them?

- "At the end of every three years, bring all the tithes of that year's produce and store it in your towns so that the Levites (who have no allotment or inheritance of their own) and the foreigners, the fatherless and the widows who live in your towns may come and eat and be satisfied, and so that the Lord your God may bless you in all the work of your hands" (Deuteronomy 14:28–29).

- "If anyone is poor among your fellow Israelites in any of the towns of the land the Lord your God is giving you, do not be hardhearted or tightfisted toward them. Rather, be openhanded and freely lend them whatever they need" (Deuteronomy 15:7–8).

- "Defend the weak and the fatherless; uphold the cause of the poor and oppressed. Rescue the weak and the needy; deliver them from the hand of the wicked" (Psalm 82:3–4).

- "Do not withhold good from those to whom it is due, when it is in your power to act. Do not say to your neighbor, 'Come back tomorrow and I'll give it to you'—when you already have it with you" (Proverbs 3:27–28).

- "Speak up for those who cannot speak for themselves, for the rights of all who are destitute. Speak up and judge fairly; defend the rights of the poor and needy" (Proverbs 31:8–9).

- "Religion that God our Father accepts as pure and faultless is this: to look after orphans and widows in their distress and to keep oneself from being polluted by the world" (James 1:27).

What happens if we do not help the poor?

- "'Because the poor are plundered and the needy groan, I will now arise,' says the Lord. 'I will protect them from those who malign them'" (Psalm 12:5).

- "May he defend the afflicted among the people and save the children of the needy; may he crush the oppressor" (Psalm 72:4).

- "Do not exploit the poor because they are poor and do not crush the needy in court, for the Lord will take up their case and will exact life for life" (Proverbs 22:22–23).

- "Suppose a brother or a sister is without clothes and daily food. If one of you says to them, 'Go in peace; keep warm and well fed,' but does nothing about their physical needs, what good is it? In the same way, faith by itself, if it is not accompanied by action, is dead" (James 2:15–17).

- "If anyone has material possessions and sees a brother or sister in need but has no pity on them, how can the love of God be in that person? Dear children, let us not love with words or speech but with actions and in truth" (1 John 3:17–18).

The prophets were especially adamant about caring for the poor. Consider Isaiah 1:17: "Seek justice. Defend the oppressed. Take up the cause of the fatherless, plead the case of the widow." These are imperatives, i.e., absolute commands from God.

Ezekiel added: "Now this was the sin of your sister Sodom: She and her daughters were arrogant, overfed and unconcerned; they did not help the poor and needy" (Ezekiel 16:49). Amos warned us about those who "deprive the poor of justice in the courts" (Amos 5:12).

To summarize, the Lord said this of godly King Josiah: "'He defended the cause of the poor and needy, and so all went well. Is that not what it means to know me?' declares the Lord" (Jeremiah 22:16).

If we do not care for the least of these, we risk the judgment of God. Yet if we share the Father's heart for those in need, we position ourselves to receive the favor of God.

Earn the right to share the gospel.

Randel Everett, a longtime pastor and friend, is right: I have no right to preach the gospel to a hungry person. Jesus met physical need so he could meet spiritual need. He healed a man's blind eyes so he could heal his blind soul (John 9). He cleansed a leper's body so he could cleanse his spirit (Luke 17:19).

When we feed the hungry, we demonstrate the relevance of our message. We show them that God's love is real when our love is real.

For instance, my wife volunteered for many years at a ministry in West Dallas called Brother Bill's Helping Hand. As the "neighbors" came each week for food and other assistance, they learned that the volunteers' love for them was genuine. They often asked why these people of relative means were giving their time to such a need. Many responded to the gospel they heard and gave themselves to Christ as their Lord.

Do good to demonstrate God's grace.

When we do good, we show our culture that our faith is good. We meet felt need to meet spiritual need, earning the right to preach the gospel.

When we come together as the body of Christ—his hands and feet—and address the needs of our cities, our cities take note. When we address poverty, take care of the sick, seek justice and safety for the immigrant, demonstrate the inherent value and humanity of the imprisoned, and work alongside God regarding other such issues, the culture sees that our faith is relevant to their issues. And we show them God's love in ours.

C. S. Lewis: "If you read history you will find that the Christians who did the most for the present world were just those who thought most of the next. The Apostles themselves, who set on foot the conversion of the Roman Empire, the great men who built up the Middle Ages, the English Evangelicals who abolished the Slave Trade, all left their mark on Earth, precisely because their minds were occupied with Heaven. It is since Christians have largely ceased to think of the other world that they have become so ineffective in this. Aim at Heaven and you will get earth 'thrown in': aim at earth and you will get neither." [59]

To reach our increasingly secular culture, these principles are vital:

1. We must serve the least of these to obey the Bible.

2. We earn the right to share the gospel by demonstrating our concern for people's fates in this life rather than solely in the life to come.

3. We must do good to prove the grace of God. Then we join God at work in our world and invite others to do the same.

Our heavenly Father rejoices when a hungry person is fed regardless of whether the meal came from the hands of a Christian or a nonbeliever. Yet he can accomplish so much more through those equipped to feed the soul as well. As a nation, this is one area where we often spend far too much time debating the best practices at a national level when the greatest good would come from more people simply choosing to make their part of America a better place.

A man once told his pastor, "I would like to ask God why he doesn't do something about all the pain and suffering in the world."

"Why don't you ask him?" his pastor replied.

"Because I'm afraid he'll ask me the same question."

God is asking, and the culture is watching.

What will be our answer?

7

Doubting that racism exists: Why the fight against racism has always been biblical

"No one is born hating another person because of the color of his skin, or his background, or his religion. People must learn to hate, and if they can learn to hate, they can be taught to love." —Nelson Mandela

According to a 2017 Gallup poll, 42 percent of Americans worry a "great deal" about race relations in the US, up 7 percent from 2016 and a record high in Gallup's seventeen-year polling trend. It was the third straight year Americans said they increasingly worry about this issue.[60]

A generation after the 1954 *Brown* school desegregation decision, the Civil Rights Act of 1964, and the Voting Rights Act of 1965, racial discrimination continues in our country. According to the FBI, 57 percent of hate crimes are racially motivated.[61] Hate groups are active in every state in America.[62]

Scripture is clear that this sin grieves the heart of God and goes directly against how he wants his people to live.

Racism and indigenous Americans

The *Oxford English Dictionary* defines *racism* as "prejudice, discrimination, or antagonism directed against someone of a different race based on the belief that one's own race is superior."[63]

By this definition, mistreating people of a particular race is "racism" to the degree that the perpetrator considers his or her victims to be racially inferior. We have found such attitudes on the part of Anglos toward non-Anglos since Europeans first landed in the New World.

Many European explorers characterized the indigenous peoples they encountered as "heathen" and considered their race and culture to be inferior by nature. Many claimed that such people could be transformed by the introduction of Christianity and European customs.

One colonist described native Americans as "having little of Humanitie but shape, ignorant of Civilitie, of Arts, of Religion; more brutish than the beasts they hunt, more wild and unmanly than the unmanned wild Countrey, which they range rather than inhabite; captivated also to Satans tyranny in foolish pieties, mad impieties, wicked idlenesse, busie and bloudy wickednesse." [64]

Racism and Africans

Many who supported the enslavement of Africans likewise viewed them as inferior to white people.

An Anglican minister in Barbados claimed that "*Negro's* were Beasts, and had no more Souls than Beasts." [65] Africans were considered intellectually and morally inferior to whites; some declared that they were descended from apes.

Such horrific claims were used to justify the system of chattel slavery (the personal ownership of a slave) that enslaved millions of Africans. Many slaveholders convinced themselves that slaves, due to their supposedly inferior nature, were better off and better cared for in bondage than in freedom.

This racist ideology led directly to America's "original sin," the institution of slavery in the New World.

The first group of African slaves—four men and women—arrived at Jamestown, Virginia, in 1619. Planters quickly realized that enormous profits could be gained from importing enslaved laborers.

Africans could be made to work much longer and harder in the fields. Since they were so far from Africa, they could not easily escape and return home. In addition, African slaves came from a variety of nations and cultures and thus could not easily communicate with each other to organize resistance.

Most slaves came from West Africa, where some tribal leaders were willing to capture and sell other Africans for profit. Slaves became especially important to the economy of the South, where the climate and topography were more suitable for tobacco and cotton plantations.

By 1860, the United States was divided into "slave" and "free" states. That year, census takers counted 3,950,540 slaves in America.[66]

While the Declaration of Independence claimed that "all men are created equal," the US Constitution determined that enslaved persons would be counted as "three-fifths of all other Persons" for purposes of government representation and taxation (Article I, Section II, Paragraph III).

The Constitution permitted importing slaves until 1808, with a tax of ten dollars per slave (Article I, Section IX, Clause I). And it required those living in free states to return escaped slaves to their owners (Article IV, Section II, Clause III).

Slavery was legal in America until 1865 and the adoption of the Thirteenth Amendment. The Fourteenth Amendment (1868) guaranteed the same rights to all male citizens; the Fifteenth Amendment (1870) made it illegal to deprive any eligible citizen of the right to vote, regardless of color.

However, segregation in schools was not made illegal until *Brown v. Board of Education* in 1954.[67] Jim Crow laws enforcing racial segregation were overturned by the Civil Rights Act of 1964 and the Voting Rights Act of 1965.

Racism and Asians

Asian immigrants have faced racial prejudice in the US as well. Those who came to America to work in mines, farms, and railroads were willing to accept lower wages, which enraged white residents.

As a result, Asians became the victims of riots and attacks. The 1882 Chinese Exclusion Act and the 1924 Asian Exclusion Act barred additional immigration. These acts also declared Asians ineligible for citizenship, which meant they could not own land. [68]

Racism today

Studies show that racism persists in America:

- People with "black-sounding names" had to send out 50 percent more job applications than people with "white-sounding names" to get a callback.

- A black man is three times more likely to be searched at a traffic stop and six times more likely to go to jail than a white man.

- If a black person kills a white person, he or she is twice as likely to receive the death sentence as a white person who kills a black person.

- Blacks serve up to 20 percent more time in prison than white people for the same crimes.

- Blacks are 38 percent more likely to be sentenced to death than white people for the same crimes. [69]

Racism persists in America's churches as well:

- Only 32 percent of white pastors strongly agree that "my church is personally involved with racial reconciliation at the local level." Fifty-three percent of African American pastors strongly agree with this statement. [70]

- Only 56 percent of evangelicals believe that "people of color are often put at a social disadvantage because of their race." Eighty-four percent of blacks agree with this statement. [71]

- A recent study showed that 86 percent of America's churches are composed of one predominant racial group. [72]

- While 90 percent of Protestant pastors say their congregation would welcome a sermon on racial reconciliation, only 26 percent say leaders in their church have encouraged them to preach on the subject. [73]

Dr. Martin Luther King Jr. was right: Sunday morning worship services are still the most segregated hour in America. And while the solution is not forced integration of the pews, actively seeking out opportunities to partner with churches that are predominately comprised of members of a different race would be a great first step in helping to desegregate the American church. After all, God's word is clear that he expects Christians of every race to work together in expanding the kingdom.

Racism and the Bible

The Bible clearly condemns all forms of racism and views every person as equally valuable. Let's look at what God's word says about our subject, then we'll consider six theological facts regarding the Scriptures and racism.

One: We are all created by God.

The human story begins in Genesis 1, where God "created mankind in his own image, in the image of God he created them; male and female he created them" (v. 27). Every person is created intentionally by God in his own divine image. Thus, every person is sacred and equally valuable. Every form of racism, by definition, is to be rejected.

Two: We are all descended from the same parents.

Every human being is descended from Adam and Eve (Genesis 1:28). As a result, "Adam named his wife Eve, because she would become the mother of all the living" (Genesis 3:20).

As Scripture notes, "From one man [God] made all the nations, that they should inhabit the whole earth" (Acts 17:26). Because of the Flood, all of humanity can trace our ancestry to Noah as well (Genesis 9:1).

Three: Every person is equally valuable to God.

Paul boldly stated, "There is neither Jew nor Gentile, neither slave nor free, nor is there male and female, for you are all one in Christ Jesus" (Galatians 3:28). This was written at a time when many Jews considered Gentiles to be unclean and inferior. Some claimed that God made Gentiles so there would be "firewood in hell." Many refused even to look upon a Gentile in public.

For their part, Gentiles persecuted the Jewish people across nearly their entire history. The Jews were enslaved by Egypt, attacked by Canaanites and other surrounding tribes, destroyed by Assyria, enslaved by Babylon, and ruled by Persia, Greece, and Rome. The Roman Empire destroyed their temple in AD 70 and disbanded their nation after the Bar Kochba revolt in AD 132–135.

Nonetheless, Scripture teaches that "there is neither Jew nor Gentile" in the eyes of God.

"There is neither slave nor free" was also a revolutionary claim. Slavery was endemic in the first-century world. Many viewed slaves, especially those who came from foreign lands, as inferior to Romans. God's word, in response, advocated for the rights and respect of slaves wherever possible, instructing God's people to treat them as one would a brother (Philemon 15–16).

"There is no male and female" was a radical statement as well. Romans considered women to be the possession of men. A female belonged to her father until she belonged to her husband. Women were either wives or concubines, with few rights of their own.

Galatians 3:28 sounds the clarion call that every form of racism known to Paul's day was invalid and sinful. The God who made us all loves us all.

Paul repeated his assertion to the Colossians: "There is no Gentile and Jew, circumcised or uncircumcised, barbarian, Scythian, slave or free, but Christ is all, and is in all" (Colossians 3:11).

To summarize: "God does not show favoritism" (Acts 10:34).

Four: Each person is equally welcome to salvation in Christ.

God loves all sinners and wants all to come to faith in his Son: "God demonstrates his own love for us in this: While we were still sinners, Christ died for us" (Romans 5:8). Our Lord "is patient with you, not wanting anyone to perish, but everyone to come to repentance" (2 Peter 3:9).

As Paul noted, God "wants all people to be saved and to come to a knowledge of the truth" (1 Timothy 2:4). That's why the apostle could testify: "I am not ashamed of the gospel, because it is the power of God that brings salvation to everyone who believes: first to the Jew, then to the Gentile" (Romans 1:16).

Our Father's saving love is available to all: "There is no difference between Jew and Gentile—the same Lord is Lord of all and richly blesses all who call on him" (Romans 10:12). His grace is universal: "For God so loved the world that he gave his one and only Son, that whoever believes in him shall not perish but have eternal life" (John 3:16).

When we trust in Christ, we become one people: "He himself is our peace, who has made the two groups one and has destroyed the barrier, the dividing wall of hostility" (Ephesians 2:14). As a result, "we were all baptized by one spirit so as to form one body—whether Jews or Gentiles, slave or free" (1 Corinthians 12:13).

Jesus "is the atoning sacrifice for our sins, and not only for ours but also for the sins of the whole world" (1 John 2:2). Peter told his fellow Jewish Christians that God "did not discriminate between us and [Gentile Christians], for he purified their hearts by faith" (Acts 15:9).

As a result, we are to "make disciples of all nations" (Matthew 28:19). "Nations" translates *ethnos*, meaning people groups. We get *ethnicity* from this word. Every person of every ethnicity is to be brought to Christ through the ministry of the church.

Surely, no one reading this book would question the fact that people of any race can be saved through faith in Christ, but it can be easy to miss the implication that all races are part of God's family. Our heavenly Father calls us to defend our brothers and sisters in Christ, regardless of their race, with the same passion and fervor that we would use to defend our biological siblings.

Think, for example, how you would react if you heard a coworker denigrating your little sister simply because she was different, or an acquaintance telling a bigoted joke at the expense of your brother because he had a different background. We should react to discrimination against our spiritual brothers and sisters in the same way. They will be with us for all eternity, a fact that should influence the way we view them today.

Five: All people will be equally valuable in paradise.

John was given this vision of heaven: "After this I looked, and there before me was a great multitude that no one could count, from every nation, tribe, people and language, standing before the throne and before the Lamb" (Revelation 7:9).

Six: We are to love all people unconditionally.

God's word is blunt: "If you show favoritism, you sin and are convicted by the law as lawbreakers" (James 2:9). "Favoritism" translates *prosopolempsia*, meaning to show partiality or prejudice, to treat one person as inherently better than another. Such prejudice is "sin."

God told his people: "The foreigner residing among you must be treated as your native-born. Love them as yourself, for you were foreigners in Egypt" (Leviticus 19:34).

Jesus taught us: "So in everything, do to others what you would have them do to you, for this sums up the Law and the Prophets" (Matthew 7:12). We are to "love your neighbor as yourself" (Matthew 22:39, quoting Leviticus 19:18).

Peter testified to the Gentiles who sought to hear the gospel: "You are well aware that it is against our law for a Jew to associate with or visit a Gentile. But God has shown me that I should not call anyone impure or unclean" (Acts 10:28).

Three common questions

One: What about the "mark of Cain"?

After Cain murdered his brother, God sentenced him to be "a restless wanderer on the earth" (Genesis 4:12). Cain protested that "I will be a restless wanderer on the earth, and whoever finds me will kill me" (v. 14).

God replied, "'Not so; anyone who kills Cain will suffer vengeance seven times over.' Then the Lord put a mark on Cain so that no one who found him would kill him" (v. 15).

The Hebrew word translated "mark" is *ot*, referring to a sign or token. It is used eighty times in the Old Testament; not once does it refer to skin color.

Nonetheless, some have identified this "mark" with being black. Since Cain was cursed for his sin against his brother, it was claimed that those whose skin was black were his descendants and were cursed by God. This claim was used to justify the enslavement of Africans.

This line of reasoning is completely wrong. As noted, the "mark" of Cain had nothing to do with his skin color. In addition, Cain's family line probably died in the Flood.

And note that Moses married a "Cushite woman" (Numbers 12:1). Cush was a region south of Ethiopia; its people were known for their black skin (Jeremiah 13:23). When Moses' brother and sister spoke against him for marrying his Cushite wife, God rebuked them (Numbers 12:4–15).

Clearly, the "mark of Cain" has nothing to do with black people.

Two: What about the "curse of Ham"?

Ham was one of Noah's three sons. Ham had four sons: Cush, Egypt, Put, and Canaan (Genesis 10:6). Ham is considered the father of black people since some of his descendants settled in Africa.

According to tradition, Cush settled in Ethiopia, south of Egypt. Egypt (also known as "Mizraim") settled in the land of Egypt. Put settled in Libya. Canaan settled above Africa and east of the Mediterranean Sea.

The Bible tells us that after the Flood, Noah became drunk (Genesis 9:21). Then "Ham, the father of Canaan, saw his father naked and told his two brothers outside" (v. 22). Shem and Japheth "covered their father's naked body" with a garment (v. 23). After Noah awoke, he said, "Cursed be Canaan! The lowest of slaves will he be to his brothers" (v. 25).

Note that Noah cursed Canaan, not Ham. Thus, his curse was irrelevant to Ham's sons who had settled in Africa and their descendants.

Also note that Noah's curse was specifically directed at Canaan, with no mention of his descendants. If Noah's curse had applied to his descendants, it would have related to the Canaanites living in the land that became Israel. It had nothing whatever to do with black people.

Nonetheless, the old *Scofield Reference Bible* of 1909 (often considered the authoritative Bible of fundamentalist Christians) interprets Genesis 9:24–25 to teach: "A prophetic declaration is made that from Ham will descend an inferior and servile posterity."[74]

With his typically brilliant exposition, Dr. Tony Evans addresses this issue, noting that biblical curses are limited to three or four generations (Exodus 20:5) and are reversed when people repent and return to obedience (Exodus 20:6). As Dr. Evans shows, Scripture consistently rebukes and rejects the claim that black people (or any other race) are inferior to any other.[75]

Three: Didn't slavery proponents use the Bible to advocate for systematic racism?

Tragically, many who supported slavery in the antebellum South used the "mark of Cain" and "curse of Ham" to justify their position. They also noted biblical statements encouraging slaves to obey their masters.

The Bible deals realistically with the practice where necessary, but it clearly endorses the intrinsic sacred value of each person. The biblical emphasis on the sanctity of life was one of the key motivating factors for William Wilberforce and others who worked so sacrificially to abolish slavery.

Like any other book, the Bible can be misused by those who misinterpret and misrepresent its teachings. For instance, when chloroform was developed, some were resistant to using it for women in childbirth since Genesis 3:16 teaches "with painful labor you will give birth to children."

When oil wells were first dug in Pennsylvania, many New York ministers opposed the project on the grounds that it would deplete the oil stored for the predestined burning of the world (2 Peter 3:10, 12). And winnowing fans (used to separate grain from chaff while farming) were rejected by Christians who thought they interfered with the providence of God since "the wind blows wherever it pleases" (John 3:8).[76]

When a doctor misuses medicine, we blame the physician, not the science. When an attorney misrepresents a legal statute, we blame the lawyer, not the law.

In responding to racists who misused the Bible to justify slavery, we should blame the racists, not the word of God.

Practical responses

God's word clearly calls us to love every person as unconditionally as he loves us. How do we put such love into practice today?

Search your own heart

A recent survey reported that 64 percent of Americans consider racism a major problem in our society and politics. Only 3 percent say it once existed but no longer does; only 1 percent say it has never been a major problem. [77]

Why is racism so pervasive and perennial in our culture?

C. S. Lewis: "If anyone would like to acquire humility, I can, I think, tell him the first step. The first step is to realize that one is proud. And a biggish step, too. At least, nothing whatever can be done before it. If you think you are not conceited, it means you are very conceited indeed." [78]

We think his logic applies to the issue of racism as well.

One reason racial discrimination is such a perennial problem is that it appeals to the core of our sin nature. In the Garden of Eden, the serpent promised the woman that, if she ate of the forbidden fruit, "you will be like God" (Genesis 3:5).

From then to now, our desire to be our own god is at the root of all our sin. As Friedrich Nietzsche noted, the "will to power" is the basic drive in human nature.

Here's our point: Racism is a way to feel superior to others on the basis of immutable realities. If I'm white and you're black, I will always be white and you will always be black. If I delude myself into believing that being white is superior to being black, I will therefore always feel superior to you.

This temptation is alluring on levels we often don't recognize. It is therefore a good first step in confronting racism to check ourselves. Ask the Holy Spirit to show you any unstated attitudes or assumptions that are discriminatory. Ask him to reveal to you any thoughts, words, or actions that are racist. And do so with the humble knowledge that every person is capable of, if not prone to, at least some racist tendencies.

Pray regularly for such discernment. And where necessary, repent.

Take the cultural initiative

"In some ways, it's super simple. People learn to be whatever their society and culture teaches them. We often assume that it takes parents actively teaching their kids, for them to be racist. The truth is that unless parents actively teach kids not to be racists, they will be." This is how Jennifer Richeson, a Yale University social psychologist, explains the continued pervasiveness of racism.

She continues: "This is not the product of some deep-seated, evil heart that is cultivated. It comes from the environment, the air all around us." Eric Knowles, a psychology professor at New York University, adds: "There's a lot of evidence that people have an ingrained even evolved tendency toward people who are in our so-called 'in group.'"[79]

What is the solution? "The only way to change bias is to change culture," according to Richeson. "You have to change what is acceptable in society. People today complain about politically correct culture, but what that does is provide a check on people's outward attitude, which in turn influences how we think about ourselves internally. Everything we're exposed to gives us messages about who is good and bad."[80]

This is one area where the culture is often ahead of the church. Whatever one might think of the Black Lives Matter movement, for example, they have done quite a bit to raise awareness of the issue at a time when many are tempted to bunker down and wait for things to return to normal. And while their impact has somewhat faded from the cultural foreground in recent years, the issues they raised have not. The status quo of America's race relations is not acceptable, and it never has been.

God's word is clear that Christians do not have the luxury of ignoring the wrongs in our society. Christians are "the salt of the earth" and "the light of the world" (Matthew 5:13, 14). If food lacks salt, the fault is not with the food. If a dark room lacks light, the fault is not with the room.

American culture, as a whole, is trying to improve the racist tendencies that have been part of our nation's story since before we were a nation. While there is understandable disagreement on the best ways to achieve solutions, the church cannot ignore this conversation.

We must set the standard in our churches, communities, and families. We must be the change we want to see. We must take proactive, positive, initiatory steps to model the inclusive love of Jesus.

Be the church

On July 12, 2016, President George W. Bush spoke at a memorial service held in Dallas for police officers who had been killed in the line of duty. He made this remarkable point: "Americans, I think, have a great advantage. To renew our unity, we only need to remember our values. We have never been held together by blood or background. We are bound by things of the spirit, by shared commitments to common ideals."[81]

President Bush is right. Many nations find their unity in a monolithic racial heritage, culture, or history. But America has never been about such uniformity. From the beginning, we were home to Protestants and Catholics and Jews, immigrants from across Europe and around the world.

As a result, our truest unity will never be horizontal, only vertical. President Bush: "At our best, we honor the image of God we see in one another. We recognize that we are brothers and sisters, sharing the same brief moment on Earth and owing each other the loyalty of our shared humanity."

In other words, the closer we draw to our Father, the closer we draw to each other.

That's why the gospel of God's reconciling love is the only transforming answer to the challenges we face. Legislation and the civil rights movement were essential to improving the lives of those who faced legalized discrimination. But laws cannot change people. Only the Spirit can do that. As a result, Christians are on the front lines of this spiritual battle for the soul and future of our nation.

Writing for the *Washington Post*, legendary Dallas pastor Dr. Tony Evans traced our racial challenges "directly to ineffective Christians" and stated, "One of the real tragedies today is that the Church as a whole has not furthered God's light, equity, love and principles in our land in order to be a positive influence and impact for good in the midst of darkness, fear and hate."

He called for churches to unite in a "solemn assembly" with prayer and fasting, to train our members to be verbal and visible followers of Jesus, and to unite for good works in our communities. This is our "God-given role of influencing the conscience of our culture." Without it, "our country will keep spiraling downward into the depths of fear and hate." [82]

The time has come for the church to be the church.

Conclusion

Every person of every race was created by the same God in his image. Every one.

Early Christians believed this transforming truth. In the second century, Justin Martyr said of his fellow Christians: "We who hated and destroyed one another, and on account of their different manners would not live with men of a different tribe, now, since the coming of Christ, live familiarly with them, and pray for our enemies."[83]

Clement of Alexandria described the true Christian: "Through the perfection of his love he impoverishes himself that he may never overlook a brother in affliction, especially if he knows that he could himself bear want better than his brother."[84]

An early Christian named Minucius Felix told the Romans, "We love one another . . . with a mutual love, because we do not know how to hate."[85] Tertullian, a second-century theologian, reported that pagans said of Christians, "See how they love one another."[86]

Christians at various points in the church's history have already lived out the kind of inclusive equality that our culture so desperately needs.

Now it's our turn.

The culture is seeking a solution for the racism that continues to divide and denigrate our nation. Through us, Christ can show them the way.

Will we let him?

8

KILLING OURSELVES:
WHY SUICIDE ISN'T
UNPARDONABLE

In a section focusing on how Americans treat each other, we should not overlook the way we treat ourselves. This issue leads us directly to the epidemic of suicide today.

Please note: If you or someone you know is struggling with suicide, read "Help for those considering suicide" located in the appendix of this book. Those who wrestle with this issue should never put off seeking help. And this issue looms large for far too many today.

Anxiety is escalating in our culture. According to recent surveys, more Americans than ever before are stressed, depressed, and anxiety-ridden.[87] Nearly forty million people in the US (18 percent) experience an anxiety disorder in any given year. Anxiety disorders are the most common and pervasive mental disorders in America.[88]

There is a direct link between anxiety and opioid use.[89] Those suffering from anxiety are two to three times more likely to have an alcohol or other substance abuse disorder.[90] Anxiety is linked to heart disease, chronic respiratory disorders, and gastrointestinal disorders.[91]

And numerous studies have related anxiety directly to suicide. Compared to those without anxiety, patients with anxiety disorder were more likely to have suicidal ideations, attempted suicides, completed suicides, or suicidal activities.[92]

As we will see, God loves us whether we love ourselves or not. He wants us to value all life as he does—including our own. The epidemic of suicide in our culture is an issue Christians should address with clarity, courage, and compassion. Only then can we help our nation become all that God wants for us.

The scope of the issue [93]

More people die from suicide than from homicide in America. According to the Centers for Disease Control and Prevention, suicide rates increased 25 percent nationally from 1999 to 2016. They rose in nearly every state.

According to the Suicide Prevention Resource Center, suicide is the second-leading cause of death for Americans ages ten to thirty-four. [94] Suicide rates are much higher in the elderly American population than for any other age group. [95]

Suicide rates have grown exponentially for women since 1999. [96] And white, middle-aged men account for 70 percent of all suicides each year. [97]

The CDC reports that more than half of the people who died by suicide did not have a known mental health condition. [98] Factors contributing to suicide include relationship problems, a crisis in the past or upcoming two weeks, problematic substance abuse, physical health problems, job or financial problems, criminal or legal problems, and loss of housing.

However, other studies have found much higher rates of mental health disorders among people at high risk of suicide. "The reason most suicide decedents don't have a known mental disorder is that they were never diagnosed, not that they didn't have one," according to one psychiatry professor. [99]

These are some of the facts regarding the tragedy of suicide. However, if you are reading this chapter because this subject is more personal than objective for you, I hope the following discussion is helpful.

I am writing as a theologian and a minister, not a counselor, psychologist, or psychiatrist. I will offer a brief overview of our subject from a biblical and theological perspective, with some practical suggestions at the conclusion of our conversation.

But if suicide is a real issue for you, I urge you to seek professional help immediately.

In this chapter we will consider:

- The history of suicide
- The Bible and suicide
- Suicide and the Catholic Church
- Suicide and the "unpardonable sin"
- God's grace when we suffer
- Three biblical promises

The history of suicide

The term *suicide* is traced in the *Oxford English Dictionary* to 1651; its first occurrence is apparently in Sir Thomas Browne's *Religio Medici*, written in 1635 and published in 1642. Before it became a common term, expressions such as "self-murder" and "self-killing" were used to describe the act of taking one's own life.

In Greek and Roman antiquity, suicide was accepted and even seen by some as an honorable means of death and the attainment of immediate salvation. Stoics and others influenced by them saw suicide as the triumph of an individual over fate. Socrates' decision to take his own life rather than violate the state's sentence of execution influenced many to see the act as noble. However, he also made clear that we belong to the gods and cannot end our lives unless they wish it so (Plato, *Phaedo* 62bc).

Many of the early Christians knew they would likely die for their faith but chose to follow Christ at any cost. These deaths are not typically considered "suicide" since they were not initiated by the person but accepted as a consequence of his or her commitment to Jesus.

Augustine (AD 354–430) was a strong opponent of any form of self-murder (cf. *City of God* 1:4–26). He appealed to the sixth commandment and its prohibition against murder. And he agreed with Socrates that our lives belong to God so that we have no right to end them ourselves. Over time, many in the church came to see self-murder as an unpardonable sin (see the discussion of the Catholic Church's position below).

In the nineteenth century, social scientists began to view suicide as a social issue and a symptom of a larger dysfunction in the community and/or home. Medical doctors began to identify depression and other disorders behind the act. Suicide became decriminalized so that the individual could be buried, his family not disinherited, and a survivor not prosecuted.

Many are confused about this difficult subject, as our society and its churches have adopted such a wide variety of positions on it. So, let's discuss biblical teachings on the issue, the Catholic position, a Protestant response, and practical help for those dealing with this tragic issue.

The Bible and suicide

God's word does not use the word *suicide*, but it has much to say on our subject.

Biblical occurrences

The Old Testament records five clear suicides:

- When Abimelech was mortally wounded by a woman who dropped a millstone on his head, he cried to his armor-bearer to kill him so his death would not be credited to the woman (Judges 9:54).

- The mortally wounded King Saul fell upon his own sword lest the Philistines abuse him further (1 Samuel 31:4).

- Saul's armor-bearer then took his own life as well (1 Samuel 31:5).

- Ahithophel hanged himself after his advice was no longer followed by King David's son Absalom (2 Samuel 17:23).

- Zimri set himself afire after his rebellion failed (1 Kings 16:18).

Additionally, some consider Jonah to have attempted suicide (Jonah 1:11–15). And Samson destroyed the Philistine temple, killing himself and all those with him (Judges 16:29–30). But many do not see this as a suicide as much as an act of military bravery.

The death of Judas is the only clear example of suicide in the New Testament (Matthew 27:3–10). Paul later prevented the suicide of the Philippian jailer and won him to Christ (Acts 16:27–28).

Some consider Jesus' death to have been a kind of suicide since he made clear: "No one takes [my life] from me, but I lay it down of my own accord" (John 10:18). However, as the divine Son of God, he could only have been killed, by any means, with his permission.

Biblical principles

God's word makes clear the sanctity of life:

- "You shall not murder" (Exodus 20:13).

- "This day I call the heavens and the earth as witnesses against you that I have set before you life and death, blessings and curses. Now choose life, so that you and your children may live" (Deuteronomy 30:19).

- "The Lord gave and the Lord has taken away; may the name of the Lord be praised" (Job 1:21).

- "Do you not know that your bodies are temples of the Holy Spirit, who is in you, whom you have received from God? You are not your own; you were bought at a price. Therefore honor God with your bodies" (1 Corinthians 6:19–20).

- "No one ever hated their own body, but they feed and care for their body, just as Christ does the church" (Ephesians 5:29).

There are times when believers may have to give their lives in the service of Christ and his kingdom (cf. Mark 8:34–36; John 13:37; Philippians 1:21–22). But voluntary martyrdom is not usually considered suicide.

As we have seen, our postmodern culture claims that absolute truth does not exist (note that this is an absolute truth claim). In a nontheistic or relativistic society, it is difficult to argue for life and against suicide. If we are our own "higher power," we can do with our lives what we want, or so we're told.

But if God is the Lord of all that is, he retains ownership over our lives and their days. He is the only one who can determine when our service is done, our intended purpose fulfilled. It is the clear and consistent teaching of Scripture that our lives belong to their Maker and that we are not to end them for our own purposes.

Suicide and the Catholic Church

Does this fact mean that suicide costs Christians their salvation? Many of the theological questions people ask in this regard relate in some way to the Catholic Church's teachings on the subject. The Catholic Catechism contains several statements regarding suicide and mortal sin (all italics are in the original).

Suicide

On suicide, the Church does not maintain that taking one's own life always leads to eternity in hell, as this statement makes clear:

#2280 Everyone is responsible for his life before God who has given it to him. It is God who remains the sovereign Master of life. We are obliged to accept life gratefully and preserve it for his honor and the salvation of our souls. We are stewards, not owners, of the life God has entrusted to us. It is not ours to dispose of (see #2281–2283).

Mortal sin

The Catholic Church maintains a distinction between "mortal" and "venial" sins. Mortal sins separate us from God's grace; venial sins, while serious, do not (see #1037, #1470, #1859–1861, and #2268).

Theological principles

The following principles of Catholic theology seem clear:

- We cannot be sure of the spiritual state of the person who commits suicide. This person may be suffering from "grave psychological disturbances" which "can diminish the responsibility of the one committing suicide" (#2282). Mortal sin requires "full knowledge and complete consent" (#1859) and can be diminished by unintentional ignorance (#1860).

- Thus, the Church "should not despair of the eternal salvation of persons who have taken their own lives" (#2283).

- However, if the person was fully aware of his or her actions, without suffering "grave psychological disturbances," this person committed murder, an act that is "gravely sinful" (#2268).

- A person who commits a mortal sin and demonstrates "persistence in it until the end" goes to hell (#1037).

Since a person who commits self-murder (suicide) cannot then repent of this sin, it is logical to conclude that this person cannot be saved from hell. However, the Catechism nowhere makes this conclusion explicit.

Suicide and the "unpardonable sin"

Most Protestants do not believe that it is possible for a Christian to lose his or her salvation, even if that person commits suicide. In this section, we'll summarize biblical principles on the subject of "eternal security." Then we'll apply them to the issue of suicide.

Know what you can know

The Bible assures us, "I write these things to you who believe in the name of the Son of God so that you may know that you have eternal life" (1 John 5:13). A literal translation would be, "We can actually and with full assurance know intellectually and personally that we have eternal life." This phrase does not mean that we gradually grow into assurance, but that we can possess here and now a present certainty of the life we have already received in Jesus.

But first we must "believe in the name of the Son of God." "Believe" means more than intellectual assent—it is the biblical word for personal trust and commitment. We can assent to the fact that an airplane will fly me from Dallas to Atlanta, but we must get on board before it can. No surgeon can operate on the basis of intellectual assent—we must submit to the procedure.

If you have made Christ your Savior, you can claim the biblical fact that you "have eternal life," present tense, right now. You are already immortal. Jesus promised, "Whoever lives by believing in me will never die" (John 11:26). We simply step from time into eternity, from this life to the next.

Nowhere does the Bible say how it feels to become the child of God because our feelings can depend on the pizza we had for supper or the weather outside the window. No circumstances or events can guarantee our salvation.

It takes as much faith to believe we are Christians today as it did to become believers. We still have not seen God or proven our salvation in a test tube. If we had, we could question the reality or veracity of what we saw or thought.

Either the Bible is true, or it is false. Either God keeps his word, or he does not. He promises that if you "believe in the name of the Son of God," you "have eternal life" this moment. You cannot lose your salvation, for you are already the immortal child of God. This is the fact of God's word.

What about "falling from grace"?

Those who believe that it is possible to trust in Christ and then lose our salvation are quick to quote Hebrews 6:4–6. These interpreters assume that the text speaks of people who have experienced a genuine conversion, then "fall away" (v. 6). They typically believe that such a person needs another salvation experience. But others disagree.

Some believe that the writer is stating a hypothetical case: if genuine Christians "have fallen away," then "it is impossible" for them "to be brought back to repentance" (vv. 4, 6). Not that they can actually fall from salvation, but, if they could, they could not be saved again. Note that if the text deals with a Christian who actually falls from faith, it teaches that the person has no chance to be saved again.

Others believe that the writer is speaking not of a Christian but of someone who considers the faith, perhaps even joins a church, but then rejects Christ. If such a person persists in unbelief, he cannot then be saved. If a person claims that he once trusted Christ but does so no more, we would believe that he was never a genuine Christian.

The Bible seems clearly to teach that a Christian is forever the child of God:

- "For God so loved the world that he gave his one and only Son, that whoever believes in him shall not perish but have eternal life" (John 3:16).

- "If anyone is in Christ, the new creation has come: The old has gone, the new is here!" (2 Corinthians 5:17).

- "My sheep listen to my voice; I know them, and they follow me. I give them eternal life, and they shall never perish; no one will snatch them out of my hand. My Father, who has given them to me, is greater than all; no one can snatch them out of my Father's hand" (John 10:27–29).

- "Everyone who lives and believes in me shall never die" (John 11:26 ESV).

What about the "unpardonable sin"?

Jesus has just healed a demon-possessed man. The crowds think he might be the Messiah, but the Pharisees say that he drives out demons by the devil himself. So, Jesus responds, "Blasphemy against the Spirit will not be forgiven" (Matthew 12:31). He repeats his warning: "Anyone who speaks a word against the Son of Man will be forgiven, but anyone who speaks against the Holy Spirit will not be forgiven, either in this age or in the age to come" (v. 32).

Peter could deny Jesus, Thomas could doubt him, and Paul could persecute his followers, yet they could be forgiven. But "blasphemy against the Spirit" cannot be forgiven, now or at any point in the future. This is the "unpardonable sin."

So, what is this sin? Let's set out what we know. We know that Christians cannot commit this sin. The Bible is clear in 1 John 1:9: "If we confess our sins, he is faithful and just and will forgive us our sins and purify us from all unrighteousness." "All" means all. No sin is unpardonable for a Christian.

We know that this sin relates to the work of the Holy Spirit in regard to unbelievers. Jesus is warning the Pharisees, those who rejected him, that they are in danger of this sin. So, what does the Spirit do with non-Christians?

- He convicts them of their sin and need for salvation: "When [the Spirit] comes, he will prove the world to be in

the wrong about sin and righteousness and judgment"
(John 16:8).

- He tells them about Christ their Savior: "When the
  Advocate comes, whom I will send to you from the Father—
  the Spirit of truth who goes out from the Father—he will
  testify about me" (John 15:26).

- He explains salvation: "The person without the Spirit does
  not accept the things that come from the Spirit of God, but
  considers them foolishness, and cannot understand them
  because they are discerned only through the Spirit"
  (1 Corinthians 2:14).

- When they confess their sins and turn to Christ, the Spirit
  makes them God's children: "If anyone does not have the
  Spirit of Christ, they do not belong to Christ. . . . And if
  the Spirit of him who raised Jesus from the dead is living in
  you, he who raised Christ from the dead will also give life
  to your mortal bodies because of his Spirit who lives in you"
  (Romans 8:9, 11).

In short, the Holy Spirit leads lost people to salvation.

So, we know that it is the "unpardonable sin" to refuse the Spirit's
work in leading you to salvation. To be convicted of your sin and need
for a savior but refuse to admit it. To be presented the gospel but
reject it.

Why is this sin unpardonable? Because accepting salvation through
Christ is the only means by which our sins can be pardoned. It is
"unpardonable" to reject the only surgery that can save your life or
the only chemotherapy that can cure your cancer. Not because the
doctor doesn't want to heal you, but because he cannot. You won't let
him. You have rejected the only means of health and salvation.

The unpardonable sin is rejecting the Holy Spirit's offer of salvation
and dying in such a state of rejection. Then you have refused the only
pardon God is able to give you. Don't do that. Be sure you have made
Christ your Lord, today.

To conclude this part of our conversation: no verse of Scripture connects suicide with our eternal destiny. If this act could cause us to lose our salvation, we believe the Bible would make that fact clear. To the contrary, we can neither earn nor lose our salvation by human actions: "It is by grace you have been saved, through faith—and this is not from yourselves, it is the gift of God—not by works, so that no one can boast" (Ephesians 2:8–9).

Suicide is a tragedy for all involved, including our Father in heaven. But the Bible nowhere teaches that it costs Christians their salvation.

God's grace when we suffer

Those who consider suicide, and those who lose someone to it, often struggle with the presence of God in the midst of such pain. Why does he allow such suffering?

"How can a good God allow bad things to happen" is a problem as old as the Garden of Eden and the Flood of Noah. Christian theologians have wrestled with it all through the history of our faith. Five basic approaches have been proposed most often.

The free-will theodicy

Augustine is usually considered the greatest Christian theologian after Paul. His approach to the problem of evil and suffering (known to theologians as the issue of "theodicy") can be summarized as follows:

- God created all that is.

- All that he created is good.

- Before the Fall, evil was therefore "non-being," potential to be chosen but not yet reality.

- God created humanity with freedom of will.

- We used this freedom to choose evil.

- Our choice brought evil into existence, absolving God of blame.

There is much in Scripture to commend Augustine's approach. God gave us freedom of will (Genesis 3:15–17; Exodus 32:26; Deuteronomy 30:19; Joshua 24:15; 1 Kings 18:21). We were given this freedom so we could choose God and good (Matthew 4:10; Proverbs 1:10; 4:14; Romans 6:13; Ephesians 6:13; 2 Peter 3:17). Our free choice for wrong leads to evil (James 1:13–15; 4:1). All people are now sinners (Romans 3:23). Our sin has resulted in a fallen world (Genesis 3:17; Romans 8:22).

Whenever evil is the product of our sinful choices, Augustine's approach explains its existence without blaming God. Applied to the question of suicide, this position would remind us that the Sovereign of the universe has chosen to limit himself to our God-given freedom. If we misuse our freedom, the fault is not with God but ourselves.

However, this approach does not adequately account for innocent suffering. Augustine would argue (correctly) that a hurricane is the product of a world which "fell" because of sin. But he could not explain why it would devastate one region rather than some other part of the planet, or why so many innocent people would be affected.

A philosopher will also ask: If man was created good by nature, why did he choose to sin? If God gave us freedom of will and knew how we would choose to use it, is he not responsible for its use (at least to some degree)?

Related to suicide caused by clinical depression, this approach cannot explain why such a disease has to exist, or why it had to affect the person in question. The free-will approach helps us understand why a person who chooses to abuse alcohol might die in a drunk-driving accident. But it doesn't explain why the innocent driver of the other car had to die as well.

The spiritual warfare model

Satan is very real. He murders and lies (John 8:44). He accuses the people of God (Job 1:9–11), resists the godly (Zechariah 3:1; Matthew

13:38–39), and tempts us to sin (1 Chronicles 21:1; Matthew 4:1). He has power over unbelievers (Acts 26:18; 2 Corinthians 4:3–4). He is a "roaring lion looking for someone to devour" (1 Peter 5:8).

As a result, much of the evil and suffering in the world is attributable to his malignant work. Paul was clear: "Our struggle is not against flesh and blood, but against the rulers, against the authorities, against the powers of this dark world and against the spiritual forces of evil in the heavenly realms" (Ephesians 6:12).

However, not all suffering is the direct result of Satan's work. We live in a fallen world in which natural disasters and disease are inevitable. People misuse their free will, as we have seen. God permits some suffering for our greater good (the third approach we're about to discuss). Satan would like us to attribute all evil to him, giving him too much power, or blame nothing on him, pretending he doesn't exist.

The right approach is to ask the Lord if there is a Satanic component to our suffering and trust that God will guide us to the truth. If we are under attack, we can claim the power of God over our enemy and find victory in his Spirit and strength.

In relating this approach to the question of suicide, we can know that Satan is a "murderer from the beginning" (John 8:44). He wants to destroy us. He will use our freedom to tempt us, but he cannot make us commit suicide. The choice is still ours.

The soul-building model

Irenaeus (ca. AD 120–ca. 200) proposed an alternative approach to our problem:

- God created us to develop into a perfect relationship with himself.
- He created the world as a place for that development.
- Evil is thus necessary as a means of our spiritual development ("soul-building").

The Bible does teach that some suffering comes from God (Deuteronomy 8:5; Job 16:12; Psalm 66:11; 90:7). We know that suffering can lead to good (Job 23:10; Psalm 119:67; 2 Corinthians 4:17; Hebrews 12:11; Revelation 7:14). Suffering can lead us to repentance (Jeremiah 7:3, 5, 7) and can refine us (Psalm 66:10; Isaiah 48:10; Malachi 3:3; 1 Peter 1:7; 4:17). Pain enables us to witness to our faith in God despite the hurt (1 Peter 2:12, 15; 3:15–16). And so, God promises to use even difficult experiences for our good, to make us more like Jesus (Romans 8:28–29).

Irenaeus explains how evil could exist before Adam and Eve chose it. His approach also affirms the hope that God can redeem any suffering for his glory and our good. Problems with this approach include the fact that the "fall" it pictures is not as catastrophic as the event described in Genesis 3. The amount of evil in the world seems disproportionate to the present good; for instance, it is hard to argue that the lessening of anti-Semitism that resulted from the Holocaust justifies the horrors of that tragedy. This approach also struggles with the existence of hell since it is not a soul-building or redemptive reality.

As related to suicide, this approach may help us understand that God can redeem depression for his glory and our good. He can even use the horrific tragedy of a suicide to help people follow him in faith. He did not cause this pain, but he can use it for a greater good.

The eschatological model

"Eschatology" deals with the future. Applied to theodicy, this approach asserts that evil will be resolved in the future, making present suffering endurable and worthwhile. Jesus promised that life leads to life eternal in glory (John 14:1–6), a paradise beyond our imagination (Revelation 21:1–5). We should not consider the present sufferings worth comparing with the glory to be revealed (Romans 8:18).

As a philosophical model, this approach offers the guarantee of absolute rational understanding. We do not comprehend the purpose of suffering now, but we will one day (1 Corinthians 13:12). All our questions will be answered. All the reasons why God has permitted suffering in our lives will be clarified. Our present faithfulness will be redeemed with future reward in glory (Revelation 2:10).

This approach does not offer an explanation in the present. And some might wonder how this promise of future hope makes present courage possible. But it does promise that the questions we cannot answer today will have their answers one day.

The existential model

The last model is more practical than theoretical: God suffers as we suffer and gives us strength to withstand, and even redeem, our pain. The Bible affirms this assertion (2 Corinthians 4:1, 16; Ephesians 3:13; Hebrews 12:5; Revelation 2:3). God walks with us through the valley of the shadow of death (Psalm 23:4). He weeps as we weep (John 11:35). Jesus experienced every temptation and pain we feel (Hebrews 4:15). He is present with us now in the sufferings of life (Deuteronomy 20:1; Psalm 34:18; Isaiah 43:2; Daniel 3:24–25; 12:6–7; Acts 16:25–26).

Philosophically, this approach is not a true theodicy. It offers no real explanation for the origin or existence of suffering. But it does provide the practical assurance that our Father walks with his children through the hardest places of life and will never allow us to face more than he will give us the strength to bear (1 Corinthians 10:13).

Your Father suffers as you suffer. If you feel pain, so does he. He knows what it is to lose a child, for he lost his Son on the cross.

Practical principles

When the tragedy of suicide strikes, how can this theological discussion help us in practical ways? Here are steps to take in the worst storms of life.

First, utilize the *free-will* approach to examine the origin of this suffering. Is there sin to admit? Is this pain in some way the result of misused freedom? If you are not sure, you may ask the Father. Where sin is part of the problem, we can claim God's forgiving grace (1 John 1:9) and make restitution to others when doing so is to their good (Luke 19:8). But do not assume that suffering is always the fault of sin. Joseph, Job, and Jesus are clear evidence to the contrary.

Second, use the *soul-building* model to ask: What can you learn from this situation? How can you grow closer to God through this pain? Strive to be open to every source from which this spiritual growth can come—ask friends for counsel, seek the Spirit in prayer and Scripture, worship God even (especially) when it's hard. Stay close enough to Jesus to hear his voice and feel his transforming touch.

Third, use the *eschatological* approach to ask: How can God redeem this present suffering for future good? How can he use your witness to touch the lives of people you may not even know? How will he reward your present faithfulness in the future and in glory? You may not be able to see the future, but you can believe that it is real.

Last, utilize the *existential* model to trust God's help in the midst of your pain. Know that he loves you no matter how the world assesses or treats you. He will always be your Father if you have asked Jesus Christ to be your Lord. Nothing can take you from his hand (John 10:28). He will enable you to get through this dark night until the dawn finally comes.

Above all, make certain that you have entered a personal relationship with your Creator and Father. Be sure that you have asked him to forgive your sins and failures and to become your Lord and Savior.

This simple prayer captures the essence of a salvation commitment: "Dear Lord, thank you for loving me. Thank you for sending your Son to die on the cross to pay the penalty for my sins. I turn from them now and ask you to forgive me for them. I invite Jesus Christ into my life as my Savior and Lord. I turn my life over to him. I will live for him as long as I live. Thank you for making me your child forever. In Jesus' name, amen."

If you prayed this prayer for the first time just now, please tell a Christian you can trust. As God's child, you need to be part of his family. His church can help you grow in your faith and stand with you in the hard times of life. Whomever you trust with your decision to follow Jesus, know that you are now the child of God for all eternity.

Three biblical promises

In the appendix of his classic, *The Problem of Pain*, C. S. Lewis includes this note from physician R. Havard: "Mental pain is less dramatic than physical pain, but it is more common and also more hard to bear. The frequent attempt to conceal mental pain increases the burden: it is easier to say 'My tooth is aching' than to say 'My heart is broken.'"[100]

Let's close by claiming three promises God makes to every suffering person today.

One: You and every person you know is someone of inestimable worth.

Depression and life crises can cause us to feel that our lives are not worth living. The opposite is true. Every person on earth is someone for whom Jesus died (Romans 5:8).

In 1941, C. S. Lewis preached his famous "Weight of Glory" sermon in St. Mary's Chapel at Oxford University. In it, he stated, "There are no *ordinary* people. You have never talked to a mere mortal. Nations, cultures, arts, civilizations—these are mortal, and their life is to ours as the life of a gnat" (his emphasis).

Lewis adds: "Next to the Blessed Sacrament itself, your neighbor is the holiest object presented to your senses."[101] So are you.

Two: God loves you and wants to help.

When Elijah despaired of his life and prayed, "It is enough; now, O Lord, take away my life" (1 Kings 19:4 ESV), God provided the physical, spiritual, and emotional sustenance he needed to go on. When Jeremiah said, "Cursed be the day I was born!" (Jeremiah 20:14), God sustained his prophet.

Scripture promises: "The Lord is close to the brokenhearted and saves those who are crushed in spirit" (Psalm 34:18). Paul, who faced almost indescribable challenges (2 Corinthians 11:23–28), could proclaim, "I consider that our present sufferings are not worth comparing with the glory that will be revealed in us" (Romans 8:18).

Jesus knows your pain. He has faced everything we face (Hebrews 4:15). He cried from the cross, "My God, my God, why have you forsaken me?" (Matthew 27:46). Now he is ready to help you.

However, let me repeat that one of the most important ways the Great Physician heals is through human physicians. That's why you need to reach out to professional counselors as soon as possible. God will use them as he ministers his grace to you.

Three: You can "dwell on the heights" with God.

Paul testified that he could "take captive every thought to make it obedient to Christ" (2 Corinthians 10:5). He could do this because he lived in the power of the Holy Spirit (Ephesians 5:18).

God wants to be "the sure foundation for your times, a rich store of salvation and wisdom and knowledge" (Isaiah 33:6). The person who walks with him "will dwell on the heights" (v. 16).

You can "dwell on the heights" with your Father. This is the promise, and the invitation, of God.

Will you accept it today?

SECTION THREE

How do
Americans
relate to God?

Introduction

We've seen that God judges people by the way they treat his word and each other. The third element of his relationship with us focuses on the way we treat him.

Scripture clearly forbids idolatry in all its forms (Exodus 20:3–6). Those who deny his existence are making an idol of whatever they trust more than they trust him. They might depend on human reason, scientific advancement, material possessions, or other illusions that promise happiness and fulfillment, but each is an idol in today's culture.

A second way God judges our relationship with him focuses on our commitment to his Son. Scripture repeatedly tells us that the Son reveals the Father and is the only way to him. Skeptics today deny his existence, his deity, and/or his uniqueness.

This section will identify biblical principles and prohibitions that relate directly to our relationship with God. It will explore the worldviews and assertions of those who do not trust and serve the Lord as their Lord. And it will equip Christians to defend our commitment to the One who is the Way, the Truth, and the Life (John 14:6).

C. S. Lewis testified, "I believe in Christianity as I believe that the Sun has risen, not only because I see it, but because by it I see everything else."[102] Let's learn how to see "everything else" by the One who is the only "light of the world" (John 8:12).

9

Is God real?

One way our culture mistreats God is to deny his existence.

Scripture warns us: "Without faith it is impossible to please God, because anyone who comes to him must believe that he exists and that he rewards those who earnestly seek him" (Hebrews 11:6).

Paul stated that "since the creation of the world God's invisible qualities—his eternal power and divine nature—have been clearly seen, being understood from what has been made, so that people are without excuse" (Romans 1:20).

When people "worshiped and served created things rather than the Creator," the consequences were severe: "Because of this, God gave them over to shameful lusts" (vv. 25, 26). David adds: "The fool says in his heart, 'There is no God'" (Psalm 14:1a). With this result: "They are corrupt, their deeds are vile; there is no one who does good" (v. 1b).

In addition, Scripture repeatedly warns us against idolatry: making anyone or anything our god rather than the one true God. We are told, "You shall have no other gods before me. You shall not make for yourself an image in the form of anything in heaven above or on the earth beneath or in the waters below" (Exodus 20:3–4).

This is a very serious sin: "I, the Lord your God, am a jealous God, punishing the children for the sin of the parents to the third and fourth generation of those who hate me, but showing love to a thousand generations of those who love me and keep my commandments" (vv. 5–6).

The prophet Jonah added: "Those who cling to worthless idols turn away from God's love for them" (Jonah 2:8; cf. Leviticus 19:4; Psalm 16:4; Jeremiah 11:12).

Those who reject the existence of God clearly believe in something or someone more than they believe in the Lord. If they depend on their reason, experience, cultural trends, conventional wisdom, or other influences, they make these into idols.

So, we can conclude that rejecting idolatry by placing our faith in God is vital to the blessing of the Lord on our lives and nation. How can we defend such faith in our postmodern, secular, post-Christian culture?

God or god?

Christopher Hitchens titled his inflammatory book *god is not Great*. Throughout his writings, he referred to the Christian deity as "god." Atheist J. L. Mackie did the same thing, but at least he capitalized the name when referring to the "God" of various faith systems.[103] Hitchens refused to be so kind since he was sure that "God" doesn't exist and thus doesn't deserve capitalization.

Most Christians (and Jews and Muslims) simply assume that he's wrong. The biblical writers presupposed the existence of God, as did their readers ("In the beginning God . . ."). But this informal, unexamined belief will not do for those who question the reality of God. We cannot have a real relationship with people who do not exist except in our minds. We can have a dream, hallucination, or fantasy about them, but we'd be schizophrenic to spend much time worshiping or serving our imaginary friends.

This is precisely what atheists claim: God exists only as a dream, hallucination, or fantasy, a belief which cannot be proven or even rationally defended.

Creation without a creator?

One way to respond to people who reject the existence of God is to ask how there can be a creation without a Creator. (This argument from cosmos to Creator is known to scholars as the "cosmological argument for God's existence.") If the universe began as a Big Bang, where did the Big Bang come from? If you think life started as a cell floating in a pool of water, we can ask what or who made the water. Since we live in a world where every effect has a prior cause, it's easy for us to reason that the world came from somewhere or Someone. This "First Cause" (to use Aristotle's term) we can call God.

Unfortunately, for those of us who like this approach, it doesn't prove as much as we might think it does.

For instance, scientists say that the universe is running down (the Second Law of Thermodynamics). Someday, perhaps 10^{150} years in the future, all energy will be converted to matter and everything will collapse on itself. Scientists call this "heat death" and say that it will make the entire universe into one "black hole." This is a rather pessimistic way of stating the Third Law of Thermodynamics.

Skeptics then ask, could this be how the Big Bang started, using forces we cannot now understand? Or, looking at the universe another way, could history move as a circle rather than a line, with a succession of Big Bang expansions and contractions?

Skeptics cannot prove any of this, of course. But then, neither can we prove our belief that God made the universe. The Bible obviously says that he did and predicts that he will one day turn history into eternity (cf. 2 Peter 3:10, Revelation 21:1–5). But it would be impossible to prove these claims unless we were there at the beginning or are there at the end. And using God's word to prove God's existence is the dictionary definition of circular reasoning.

Design without a designer?

Another way to argue for God's existence begins with the design we see in our world. (Scholars call this the "teleological" argument, from the Greek *telos*, meaning "design" or "end.")

To state the argument in its classic sense, suppose you were walking in a forest and came upon a rock. You'd not be surprised to find it where it is. But suppose you walked a little farther and came upon a watch lying on the ground. You would not believe that the hands, wristband, and other components of the watch just "happened" to fall together in that place and in that way.

Is the world not infinitely more complex than a watch?

Once we start down this mental path, we can find examples of remarkable design nearly everywhere we look. In a debate with the atheist Kai Nielsen, J. P. Moreland suggested several:

> In the formation of the universe, the balance of matter to antimatter had to be accurate to one part in ten billion for the universe to even arise. Had it been larger or greater by one part in ten billion, no universe would have arisen. There would also have been no universe capable of sustaining life if the expansion rate of the Big Bang had been one billionth of a percent larger or smaller.
>
> Furthermore, the chance possibilities of life arising spontaneously through mere chance has been calculated by Cambridge astronomer Fred Hoyle as being 1 x 10.40, which Hoyle likens to the probabilities of a tornado blowing through a junkyard and forming a Boeing 747. Had these values, these cosmic constants which are independent of one another, been infinitesimally greater or smaller than what they are, no life remotely similar to ours—indeed, no life at all—would have been possible. [104]

People who are persuaded by the design argument claim that the universe is not old enough for life to have evolved naturally. According to them, the odds that our present world could have evolved by random chance are too small to be plausible, if they're even possible.

The easiest way for a skeptic to respond to this argument is to invoke Darwin's assertion that life evolves through natural selection and survival of the fittest. If this is true, life did not come to exist as a tornado through a junkyard. Rather, we evolved through a process that chose the parts necessary to make that Boeing 747. The odds of "random" or "chance" occurrence are irrelevant in a world that evolved through such a process of selection.

Some evolutionists even claim that natural selection must have created life as we know it, that the odds were much higher in favor of life than against it. It would likely have taken much longer than fifteen billion years for the universe to have evolved through random coincidence, but this is not how things happened. Natural selection "sped up" the process of creating life as we know it.

Scholars continue to debate the merits of Darwinian evolution. But whether you believe that Darwin was brilliant or deluded, you can see why atheistic evolutionists aren't impressed with the design argument.

Morality without a moral God?

A third way to argue for God's existence begins with the fact of human morality. We all have a sense of right and wrong, but why? Where did your conscience come from? "My parents," you might say. But where did your parents get theirs? And where did their parents get theirs? And so on.

Ultimately, we can reason back to a God who is holy and created the human race with a sense of morality that reflects his own.

Unfortunately, this approach is not very compelling for skeptics, either. It's easy to claim that our morality illustrates the Darwinian principle of self-preservation since it often does. Or we could credit natural selection for encouraging morality as a way of ensuring the survival of the species.

Even moral choices that seem to violate the instinct for self-preservation, such as a Christian who dies for his or her faith, can be explained as a selfish quest for admiration in this life and glory in the next. A Muslim suicide bomber seeking reward in paradise tragically illustrates the point.

Reasons not to believe

It would seem that none of the classical arguments for God's existence can compel us to believe in him. What's worse, there are several reasons to reject such faith.

First, as we have seen, evolutionary theory can be used to explain the design of the world apart from faith in a designing God.

Second, if there is actually a God who made all that exists, it would seem that we would know he is real. Noted atheist and author Sam Harris makes an apparently reasonable statement: "An atheist is simply a person who believes that the 260 million Americans (87 percent of the population) claiming to 'never doubt the existence of God' should be obliged to present evidence for his existence."[105] It shouldn't be so hard to comply with his request.

Third, some atheists go so far as to claim that the very words "God exists" are meaningless and incoherent.[106] What do we mean by "God"? We cannot point to anything in the created world since this would be idolatry, making creation into the creator. Neither can we point to anything within the rational concept of "God" since, by definition, our finite minds cannot comprehend an infinite being. If we cannot speak rationally of "God," how can we believe in him?

Fourth, the problem of innocent suffering greatly compounds things. It can be hard to believe that an all-loving, all-powerful God created a world filled with evil and suffering. As Harris makes the point, "An atheist is a person who believes that the murder of a single little girl—even once in a million years—casts doubt upon the idea of a benevolent God."[107]

Reasons to believe

So, where are we? One answer is to claim that God exists because the Bible says he does. Of course, other religious books make the same claim for themselves. The Qur'an claims that there is no God but Allah (the Arabic word for "God") and that Muhammad is his prophet. The Book of Mormon not surprisingly supports the teachings of The Church of Jesus Christ of Latter-day Saints. We'd be amazed to find a religion whose sacred writings do not advocate what the religion believes.

It helps that the Bible has such outstanding evidence for its trustworthy nature. But even considering the manuscripts, archaeological evidence, internal consistency, and fulfilled prophecy, we cannot prove that the Bible is divinely inspired or that the God it advocates actually exists.

A second response is to claim that it is reasonable to believe in God, without trying to prove our assertion. This we can certainly do. While arguing from creation to Creator or design to Designer does not prove that God exists, such thinking is clearly logical. Skeptics may not agree that we are right, but they cannot prove that we are wrong.

This fact is significant. It would obviously be a veto to the Christian faith if we could not demonstrate that believing in God is at least rational. We would have a hard time getting you to join us in worshiping Martians since no evidence could persuade you of their existence (we hope). But we can logically argue that God made and designed the world. Even if skeptics credit evolutionary natural selection as the explanation for life as we know it, they cannot prove that they are right. Their theory may be plausible, but so is ours, and the weight of evidence is such that, at the end of the day, it takes more faith to believe that God does not exist than to believe that he does.

Once we have shown that believing in God is reasonable, we can invite people to step from evidence into experience. As with all relationships, a relationship with God becomes self-validating. We know that God exists because we have experienced him. His existence was reasonable before we met him and compelling now that we have.

A third way to argue for God's existence is to ask: What else do we want God to do to prove himself? How could he have done things differently?

Consider the four attacks on his existence we noted earlier. The first was that evolutionists can point to natural selection as explaining life without a designing God. For instance, human hands typing on a computer seem similar to a chimpanzee's opening a banana. According to evolutionists, this fact proves that we come from a common ancestor. The adaptation of various species to their changing environment is further evidence of evolution at work, we're told. Similarity and adaptation show that the world could have evolved without God.

But consider the possibility that God made a world in which life can adapt to a changing environment. In that case, adaptation does not negate design—it proves it. And perhaps God wanted us to be able to type and a chimpanzee to be able to eat a banana, so he designed our hands in similar ways to perform similar functions.

Most cars have four wheels, but this doesn't mean that they all came from the same factory.

The second attack on God's existence we considered earlier argued that if God made the universe, it is reasonable to assume that we would be sure of his existence. But how? What would we like God to do that he has not already done? He made a world which bears remarkable evidence of creative power and designing genius. We can explain life through adaptation, but that very adaptation is part of his brilliant plan.

He then stepped into his creation on numerous occasions. He sent his angels to men and women. He revealed himself in dreams and visions and continues to do so today. He then entered the human race, folding omnipotence down into a fetus and becoming a man like us. He proved his divinity by rising from the grave and returning to heaven. He gave us a book that records these events in remarkable and trustworthy detail.

What more would we like him to do? He could appear to you as you read these words, just as he appeared in the flesh twenty centuries ago. But many did not believe in his divinity even when they saw his miracles and knew about his resurrection. In the same way, you could dismiss your experience as a hallucination or dream, believing that your senses were deceiving you. The only way you could be absolutely certain that God exists would be to stand in his presence on Judgment Day.

One day, you will.

Christianity can, in fact, be verified with absolute certainty. One day in the future, you will be sure beyond any shadow of a doubt that God is real and Jesus is Lord. But God is graciously giving you another day to trust in him by faith, another day to step into a personal relationship with him and experience the verification that comes to those who meet God for themselves. One day, time will run out, and every knee will bow and every tongue will confess that Jesus Christ is Lord, to the glory of God the Father (Philippians 2:10–11).

Until that day, there is nothing more a supernatural God can do to prove his existence through natural means. Asking the infinite, perfect God of the universe to prove himself to our finite, fallen minds is like asking him to make a square circle. Even God is not obligated to do what is logically impossible.

The third argument we noted earlier was that the statement "God exists" has no meaning or coherence since we cannot define "God" through experience or reason. Again, how is this God's fault? What would we have him do differently? We should not be surprised that we cannot define or describe him through his creation. Or that our finite, fallen minds cannot understand or describe him through the use of reason.

If we could, he would not be God. If our brains were simple enough for us to understand them, we would be too simple to understand them. How much more is this the case with the omnipotent Lord of the universe!

The fourth argument against God we noted earlier is the problem of innocent suffering. This tragic fact makes it understandably difficult for many to believe that an omnipotent, all-loving God exists. However, as we noted in the chapter on suicide, there are reasonable ways of responding to this challenge. We can know that God loves us no matter our circumstances today.

So, does God exist?

Does the president of the United States or the Queen of England exist? Not so that we can prove it. We can doubt every reference to them in the media. If you claim to have met them, we could refuse to believe you. Only if we met them for ourselves could we be absolutely certain that they are real.

Do love and friendship exist? We cannot prove to you that our wives love us, or that our friends are truly our friends. We could tell you about the times they have expressed their commitment to us, but you could say they are lying. We could show you all the wonderful things they do for us, but you could claim that they are manipulating and misleading us. You'd have to experience our marriages or friendships to know that they are real.

This is the nature of personal relationships, even with the God of the universe.

It seems that God has done everything he can do to prove his reality to us. The rational arguments for his existence demonstrate that faith is reasonable and logical. He has interacted with our world throughout human history and entered our race personally. He gave us a trustworthy written record of his creative work. He is available personally to everyone who is willing to trust in him. As a result, you could argue that more evidence exists for God than for Julius Caesar or George Washington.

The biggest problem atheists have with believing in God is that such faith requires them to accept the supernatural. If you are a materialist, certain that supernatural reality cannot exist, no amount of proof or persuasion will convince you of a supernatural being. Once you conclude that the world must be flat, nothing in logic or experience can prove you wrong. The presupposition determines the conclusion.

Of course, believing that the supernatural cannot exist is a belief. Materialism is a faith commitment. A materialist cannot prove that the supernatural does not exist, any more than a supernaturalist can prove that it does. The best we can do is to examine the evidence and then make a decision that transcends it. You'll know God is real when you ask him to be real in you.

Conclusion (by Dr. Jim Denison)

It has been my privilege to travel frequently to Cuba over the years, speaking in Cuban churches and falling in love with the Cuban people. Cuban Christians are among the most gracious, joyous, and persecuted people I've ever known. When Cubans make public their faith and are baptized as Christians, everything changes. They are assigned to the worst jobs; their children get the hardest military assignments; their families are followed, harassed, and sometimes much worse. Such is life for a believer in a country whose government is officially atheistic.

Despite such daily opposition, the Christians I have met in Cuba worship God with passion and serve him with great delight. I've seen them stand on their feet for three hours in the heat of the summer, singing their praise to the Lord. Some ride bikes or walk many miles to get to church services. They hold Bible studies in their homes and share their meager possessions with those even poorer than themselves. Their love for Jesus both shames and encourages me.

Baptism is an especially significant time for them. This is when they declare to the government and the world that they follow Jesus. This is when their society marks them as Christians and treats them accordingly. Baptism is their entrance into a world of constant persecution.

During one of my trips to Cuba, I was invited to participate in a mass baptism service. Despite the suffering they would face, more than one hundred new believers decided to take this step of public obedience. The church's baptistery was not nearly large enough for the crowd, so we traveled by flatbed trucks and open buses to a lake on the outskirts of the town.

Each of us who were baptizing waded out thirty or so feet into the shallow lake, then turned to face the crowd gathered at the bank. Soon, candidates began sloshing out to us. The first person I was to baptize was a young woman being carried through the water by a man I presumed to be her husband.

I was surprised that she wasn't walking on her own, as the lake was not very deep, and assumed that she was afraid of the water. He handed her to me. I took her in my arms, spoke the baptismal declaration over her, and immersed her. When she came up out of the water, the joy on her face was beyond description. She shouted "Hallelujah!" and raised her arms victoriously into the air.

I handed her back to her husband, who took her in his arms. When he did, he raised her up out of the lake. Then I saw that she had only one leg.

Surviving in her society with such a disability would be challenging enough for anyone. Doing so as a baptized Christian would make her life difficult beyond belief. But if you had seen her face and felt her joy, you wouldn't wonder if God was real in her life and soul.

Or if he could be real in yours.

10

Is Jesus really God?

"Whoever does not honor the Son does not honor the Father, who sent him" (John 5:23).

These words from Jesus make clear the fact that we must believe in the Son to have a relationship with the Father. As we will see in the next chapter, faith in Christ is the only way to experience eternal life.

A prior question to the uniqueness of Jesus, however, concerns his existence and divinity. An increasingly popular claim by skeptics today is that Jesus of Nazareth never existed, or, if he did, he was not God.

Why should you believe that Jesus is God? No other religion does. What makes Christians right and everyone else wrong?

If we're wrong about Jesus, we're wrong about the belief that is most central to our faith. If Muslims were proven wrong about Muhammad or Buddhists about Buddha, we wouldn't be very impressed with their religion. It would be hard for skeptics to make Jesus their Lord if they're not sure about Jesus.

So, how can we defend the existence and deity of Jesus today?

Is there non-Christian evidence for Jesus?

If Jesus is really God, it would seem that we wouldn't need the New Testament to tell us so. Non-Christians writing during the early years of the Christian movement surely would have known something about him.

In fact, they did.

If you refused to open a New Testament, what could we tell you about Jesus? Everything you would need to know to trust in him as your Lord. If we had no New Testament, we could defend the belief that Jesus is Lord solely on the basis of non-Christian writings, which are nearly all as old as the New Testament books themselves.

Here is a brief survey of the evidence, presented in chronological order.

Thallus the Samaritan (AD 52) wrote a work tracing the history of Greece from the Trojan War to his own day. In it, he attempts to explain the darkness of the crucifixion of Jesus as an eclipse of the sun. This is the earliest pagan reference to Jesus' existence and death.

Mara bar Serapion (writing after AD 70, as he describes the Fall of Jerusalem) adds: "What advantage did the Jews gain from executing their wise King? It was just after that their kingdom was abolished." His letter is on display in the British Museum today. It shows that the first Christians saw Jesus not just as a religious teacher, but as their King.

The Roman historian Suetonius (AD 65–135) records: "Punishments were also inflicted on the Christians, a sect professing a new and mischievous religious belief" (*Nero* 16.2). Note that the Empire would not punish people who followed a religious teacher, only one who made him Lord in place of Caesar.

Tacitus (AD 55–120) was the greatest ancient Roman historian. Around AD 115, he wrote, "Christus . . . suffered the extreme penalty during the reign of Tiberius at the hands of one of our procurators, Pontius Pilatus, and a most mischievous superstition broke out" (*Annals* 15.44).

His description of the Christian faith as "superstition" shows that Tacitus considered the followers of "Christus" to believe something supernatural or miraculous, not simply that he was a great human teacher. And it proves the New Testament record that Jesus was crucified by Pontius Pilate.

Pliny the Younger was a Roman administrator, author, and governor of Bithynia in Asia Minor. Two volumes of his letters still exist today.

The tenth of his correspondence books (written around AD 112) contains the earliest non-biblical description of Christian worship: "They were in the habit of meeting on a certain fixed day before it was light, when they sang in alternate verses a hymn to Christ as to a god." Note that believers worshiped Christ as God in AD 112, not centuries later after their beliefs "evolved," as some critics claim.

Flavius Josephus, the noted Jewish historian (AD 37/38–97), records: "Ananias called a Sanhedrin together, brought before it James, the brother of Jesus who was called the Christ, and certain others . . . and he caused them to be stoned" (*Antiquities* 20.9.1). Thus, early Christians called Jesus the Christ, the Messiah. Again, this was centuries before Constantine and the so-called evolution of the faith (as we will see below).

Finally, consider Josephus' most famous statement about Jesus (*Antiquities* 18.3.3):

> Now, there was about this time, Jesus, a wise man, if it be lawful to call him a man, for he was a doer of wonderful works, a teacher of such men as receive the truth with pleasure. He drew over to him both many of the Jews, and many of the Gentiles. He was Christ; and when Pilate, at the suggestion of the principal men amongst us, had condemned him to the cross, those that loved him at the first did not forsake him, for he appeared to them alive again the third day, as the divine prophets had foretold these and ten thousand other wonderful things concerning him; and the tribe of Christians, so named from him, are not extinct at this day.

While most historians do not believe that this paragraph represents Josephus' own faith, it does document the beliefs of early Christians regarding Jesus. And note that it was written before the end of the first century.

So, from these early non-Christian records we know that Jesus Christ existed, that he was crucified, and that the first Christians believed that he was raised from the dead and worshiped him as Lord. These are the facts of the gospel. And we can be sure of them without opening a Bible.

What did the earliest Christians believe?

Some claim that the divinity of Jesus was developed over centuries by the church. In addition to the non-biblical evidence we've just considered, it is easy to know what the early Christians thought of Jesus. His earliest followers would be shocked to hear the accusation that the church transformed the earthly Jesus into the divine Christ.

For instance, the *Didache*, written before AD 100, repeatedly called Jesus "the Lord." It ends thus: "The Lord shall come and all his saints with him. Then shall the world 'see the Lord coming on the clouds of Heaven'" (16.7–8). Clement of Rome, writing in AD 95, repeatedly referred to the "Lord Jesus Christ." And he promised a "future resurrection" that God will produce on the basis of his "raising the Lord Jesus Christ from the dead" (24.1).

Ignatius, writing between AD 110 and 115, referred to "Jesus Christ our God" (introduction to his letter to the Ephesians). To the Smyrnaeans he added, "I give glory to Jesus Christ, the God who has thus given you wisdom" (1.1). And Justin the Martyr (ca. AD 150), repeatedly referred to Jesus as the Son of God (cf. *Apology* 22). He was convinced that God raised him from the dead and brought him to heaven (*Apology* 45).

The Roman Empire would have considered followers of a mere rabbi to be no threat to its power. And yet, that empire persecuted Christians to the death. Why? Because they claimed no king but the Lord Jesus and would worship no god but him.

The radical faith and courage of the first apostles and the rapid spread of the Christian movement cannot be explained except by the fact that the living Lord Jesus changed their lives and empowered their witness. Multiplied thousands died because of their commitment to him.

Did Jesus claim to be God?

In recent years, many skeptics have claimed that Jesus of Nazareth saw himself only as a religious teacher and that the church deified him over the centuries. Not according to the eyewitnesses.

When Jesus stood on trial for his life, the high priest challenged him: "I charge you under oath by the living God: Tell us if you are the Messiah, the Son of God" (Matthew 26:63). His answer sealed his fate: "Yes. It is just as you say" (v. 64 NIRV). Earlier he told his opponents, "Before Abraham was, I am" (John 8:58). He clearly claimed to be God.

The gospels record further evidence in Jesus' own words:

- "Heaven and earth will pass away, but my words will never pass away" (Matthew 24:35).

- "As the Father has life in himself, so he has granted the Son also to have life in himself. And he has given him authority to judge because he is the Son of Man" (John 5:26–27).

- "'My Father is always at his work to this very day, and I too am working.' For this reason they tried all the more to kill him; not only was he breaking the Sabbath, but he was even calling God his own Father, making himself equal with God" (John 5:17–18).

I'm not sure what Jesus could have said to make clearer the fact that he was God. It won't work to counter that these statements were composed by the church as it tried to deify Jesus since they were written when eyewitnesses to his earthly life were still living.

C. S. Lewis makes the point clearly. Consider the most famous words of this famous book:

I am trying here to prevent anyone saying the really foolish thing that people often say about Him: 'I'm ready to accept Jesus as a great moral teacher, but I don't accept His claim to be God.' That is the one thing we must not say. A man who was merely a man and said the sort of things Jesus said would not be a great moral teacher. He would either be a lunatic—on a level with the man who says he is a poached egg—or else he would be the Devil of Hell. You must make your choice. Either this man was, and is, the Son of God: or else a madman or something worse. You can shut Him up for a fool, you can spit at Him and kill Him as a demon; or you can fall at His feet and call Him Lord and God. But let us not come with any patronizing nonsense about His being a great human teacher. He has not left that open to us. He did not intend to.[108]

Note again that Christians were claiming divinity for Jesus during a time when eyewitnesses to his life would quickly have contradicted them if they were wrong. For instance, consider Paul's summary of the Christ event:

What I received I passed on to you as of first importance: that Christ died for our sins according to the Scriptures, that he was buried, that he was raised on the third day according to the Scriptures, and that he appeared to Cephas, and then to the Twelve. After that, he appeared to more than five hundred of the brothers and sisters at the same time, most of whom are still living, though some have fallen asleep. Then he appeared to James, then to all the apostles (1 Corinthians 15:3–7).

Scholars believe that Paul "received" this statement from other Christians between three and eight years after the crucifixion itself, then included it in his first letter to the Corinthians. If Paul received it at such an early date, the creed must have been written even earlier. For all practical purposes, this statement must have been composed when the original events occurred.[109] In addition, it has been proven that it takes more than two generations, and usually much longer, for an event to become a myth.[110]

Jesus' first followers were completely committed to the truth of his claims to divinity. Consider the implausibility of this claim. The only Son of God, existing before time began, ruling the universe alongside the only God and Father of all creation, chose to enter the world during their lifetime.

He was the only baby to choose his parents, yet he chose a peasant teenager for his mother and a poor Galilean carpenter to be his earthly father. He was the only baby to arrange the circumstances of his birth, yet he chose a cave behind a crude travelers inn outside a tiny country town, with only dirt-caked field hands to witness his entrance into the human race.

He then grew up in a village so small it is not named even once in the entire Old Testament. He picked fishermen and tax collectors to be his disciples. He died as a convicted felon on a cross. Then he came back to life and ascended into heaven. It's all too incredible to be imagined.

And yet Peter and the other apostles refused to stop preaching these very claims, even when threatened with their lives (cf. Acts 5:29–32). While there were at least fifty tombs of holy men that became sites of religious veneration during the time of Jesus, there is no evidence that Christians ever venerated the tomb of their Lord, for the simple reason that it was empty.[111] Each apostle but John was martyred for serving this Lord, and John was exiled to the prison island of Patmos for preaching about him. Billions of people across twenty centuries have accepted the claims of these first Christians and have followed their Lord as the God of the universe.

How do we know he was right?

So, Jesus claimed to be God, and his early followers believed him. But Muslims believe the testimony of Muhammad, while Buddhists believe the teachings of Buddha. Is there any objective evidence that Christians are right about Christ?

Here is the rope from which Christianity swings, the one fact which makes or breaks our faith: "If there is no resurrection of the dead, then not even Christ has been raised. And if Christ has not been raised, our preaching is useless and so is your faith. More than that, we are then found to be false witnesses about God, for we have testified about God that he raised Christ from the dead. But he did not raise him if in fact the dead are not raised" (1 Corinthians 15:13–15).

We have seen the evidence that Jesus existed and was crucified at the hands of Pontius Pilate. We know that the first Christians believed him to be raised from the dead. Before Easter, the disciples were sure that their leader was dead and gone. After that day, they were transfused with divine courage and set about winning the world to Jesus. But believing doesn't make it so. Is there objective evidence for their faith in a risen Savior?

David Hume was an eighteenth-century Scottish philosopher known today as the "Father of Skepticism." He made it his life's work to debunk assumptions he considered unprovable, among them belief in miracles. He suggested six criteria by which we should judge those who claim to have witnessed a miracle. Such witnesses should be:

- Numerous

- Intelligent

- Educated

- Of unquestioned integrity

- Willing to undergo severe loss if proven wrong

- And their claims should be capable of easy validation. [112]

These criteria are an excellent way to determine the truthfulness of a witness. How do the eyewitnesses to the risen Christ fare by them?

These witnesses were *numerous*: over five hundred saw the resurrected Lord (1 Corinthians 15:6). They were *intelligent* and *well-educated*, as the books they wrote make clear.[113] Paul was, in fact, trained by Gamaliel, the finest scholar in Judaism (Acts 22:3). They were men and women of *unquestioned integrity*, clearly *willing to undergo severe loss*, as proven by their martyrdoms. And their claims were *easily validated*, as witnessed by the empty tomb anyone could view (cf. Acts 26:26: "It was not done in a corner.").

So, the witnesses were credible. But is there objective evidence for their claims? It is a fact of history that Jesus of Nazareth was crucified and buried, and that, on the third day, his tomb was found empty. Skeptics have struggled to explain his empty tomb ever since.

Three of their strategies centered on theft. The first claimed that Jesus' disciples stole his body while the guards at the tomb slept (Matthew 28:11–15). But how would sleeping guards know the identity of these thieves? How could the disciples convince five hundred people that the corpse was alive? And why would these disciples then die for what they knew to be a lie?

A second approach claims that the women stole the body. But how would they overpower the guards? How would they make a corpse look alive? Why would they suffer and die for such fabrication?

A third explanation is that the authorities stole the body. When the misguided disciples found an empty tomb, they mistakenly announced a risen Lord. But why would the authorities steal the body they had stationed guards to watch? When Christians began preaching the resurrection, wouldn't they quickly produce the corpse?

A fourth approach is the wrong-tomb theory: the grief-stricken women and apostles went to the wrong tomb, found it empty, and began announcing Easter. But the women saw where he was buried (Matthew 27:61); Joseph of Arimathea, the owner of the tomb, would have corrected the error (Matthew 27:57–61); and the authorities would have gone to the correct tomb and produced the corpse.

A fifth strategy is the "swoon theory": Jesus did not actually die on the cross. He or his followers bribed the medical examiner to pronounce him dead, then he revived in the tomb and appeared to be resurrected. But how could he have survived the spear thrust into his side or the burial clothes that would have smothered him? In his emaciated condition,[114] how could he have shoved aside the stone and overpowered the Roman guards? How could he have appeared through walls (John 20:19, 26) and then ascended to heaven (Acts 1:9)?

There is only one reasonable explanation for the empty tomb, the changed lives of the disciples, and the overnight explosion of the Christian movement upon the world stage: Jesus Christ rose from the dead. He is therefore the person he claimed to be: our Lord and God. He was justified in making the most stupendous claim in human history, one repeated by no other individual in all of recorded history: "All authority in heaven and on earth has been given to me" (Matthew 28:18). With this result: "Therefore go and make disciples of all nations" (v. 19).

So, is Jesus God?

You've now surveyed the basic arguments for the divinity of Jesus, looking both at non-biblical and biblical evidence. You have seen proof outside the Bible that Jesus existed and that the first Christians worshiped him as their risen Lord. You have considered the improbability that the earliest believers would have risked everything for a message they knew to be a lie. You have looked at every logical explanation for the empty tomb.

Still, don't you wish there were more? If Jesus of Nazareth were really the Son of God in the flesh, wouldn't you assume that the entire world would know it? Wouldn't you expect absolute proof that God visited our planet?

We understand such sentiments, and we share them. But, as we noted in wrestling with the existence of God, we need to step back and ask what more we could ask God to do than he has done.

He sent his Son to join the human race, miraculously announcing the event with an angelic chorus and virgin birth. This Son lived a perfect, sinless life. He performed miracles never before seen in human history. He was crucified in full public view, buried in a guarded grave, and raised from the dead on the third day.

His critics have never been able to explain his empty tomb. He appeared alive to more than five hundred people, then ascended to heaven in full view of more than one hundred. He gave us a New Testament to transmit this information to the world and preserved its text with remarkable and trustworthy accuracy.

Suppose God did it all again in our lifetime so we wouldn't have to depend on ancient records and evidence. Would our response be any different from that of his first eyewitnesses? Some would believe that his miracles and resurrection were real, but others would not. He could appear at your side as you read this book, but you could decide that your senses were deceiving you.

If we don't believe that miracles are possible, no miracle can convince us otherwise.

Conclusion (by Dr. Jim Denison)

I remember visiting my Aunt Daisy and Aunt Clara when I was a child. These sisters lived together in Buffalo, Missouri, and must have been the reason Missouri is called the "Show-Me State." More hardened skeptics the world has never seen. Aunt Daisy and Aunt Clara were certain that the government was not to be trusted, that television news was fabricated, and that newspapers were fiction. If they didn't see it, they didn't believe it.

They were especially dubious about televised reports that men had landed on the moon. They told all who would listen that NASA had staged the whole thing on some sand dunes in Arizona and had kept the money. I remember asking them about the moon rocks I'd seen in a museum.

"How do you know they're really from the moon?" they countered.

It's a good question.

My aunts grew up in a day when space flights were the stuff of comic-book fantasy. Everyone knew that it was impossible to go into space. So, there was absolutely no evidence on television or in the papers that could convince my aunts that men had actually walked on the moon. I suppose the only way they could have been persuaded would have been to fly them to the moon. If any eighty-year-old women could have made the trip, it would have been my Aunt Daisy and Aunt Clara.

That's how it is with faith in Jesus. No reporters, biblical or contemporary, can prove his divinity beyond any doubt. But when your physical life comes to its end, you will be absolutely, 100 percent certain about the divinity of Jesus Christ. Before that time comes, you'll have to take it on faith.

To believe in his divinity is a faith commitment. Not to believe in his divinity is a faith commitment. I am convinced that the evidence strongly endorses the former. And I can tell you that my personal relationship with Jesus Christ proves to me that he is risen and alive. But the only way you can be sure is to meet him for yourself.

The Son of God would like nothing better.

II

Is Jesus the only way to God?

In this section, we have noted that a people blessed by God must believe that he exists and that Jesus is his divine Son. A third question now stands before us: Is Jesus the only way to God?

Here we encounter the issue of pluralism: belief in many gods. Since our postmodern culture denies absolute truth and biblical authority, claiming that tolerance is the highest value, we can see why tolerating all religions as equally valid (or invalid) would be popular.

According to the Pew Research Center, 65 percent of Americans say that "many religions can lead to eternal life." Unfortunately, the same percentage of religiously affiliated Americans say the same. Eighty-four percent of white Catholics and 82 percent of white mainline Protestants agree. [115]

What does the Bible say about such "tolerance"?

The Word of God and belief in many gods

The Old Testament

The Old Testament strongly warns us against such heresy. Here are just a few examples:

- "Whoever sacrifices to any god other than the Lord must be destroyed" (Exodus 22:20).
- "Do not invoke the names of other gods; do not let them be heard on your lips" (Exodus 23:13).

- "Do not make a covenant with [the Canaanites] or with their gods" (Exodus 23:32).

- Speaking of the Jewish people, Moses declared: "They sacrificed to false gods, which are not God—gods they had not known, gods that recently appeared, gods your ancestors did not fear. . . . The Lord saw this and rejected them because he was angered by his sons and daughters" (Deuteronomy 32:17, 19).

- "Fear the Lord and serve him with all faithfulness. Throw away the gods your ancestors worshiped beyond the Euphrates River and in Egypt, and serve the Lord" (Joshua 24:14).

- "Do not forget the covenant I have made with you, and do not worship other gods" (2 Kings 17:38).

The New Testament

The New Testament is equally adamant that Jesus is the only way to the Father:

- Jesus said to his followers, "Whoever rejects me rejects him who sent me" (Luke 10:16).

- Our Lord warned the crowds, "Whoever is not with me is against me, and whoever does not gather with me scatters" (Luke 11:23).

- He also stated, "Whoever does not honor the Son does not honor the Father, who sent him" (John 5:23).

- "Every spirit that acknowledges that Jesus Christ has come in the flesh is from God, but every spirit that does not acknowledge Jesus is not from God" (1 John 4:2–3).

John 14

John 14 is an especially pivotal chapter in this context. Here we find four crucial facts.

First, *Jesus alone claimed divinity*. In John 14:9 he asserted, "Anyone who has seen me has seen the Father." Earlier the authorities tried to stone him to death specifically because he claimed to be God (John 10:33).

Other religious leaders have claimed to reveal God; Jesus alone claims to be God. It would be blasphemy for a Muslim to say that Muhammad was God. Buddha never claimed to be God, and, in fact, taught that there is no personal God. No one in Hindu or Jewish history every claimed to be God. But Jesus did.

Second, *Jesus is preparing our place in heaven* (John 14:2). Other religious leaders taught about heaven or the afterlife; Jesus alone claims to be preparing it for us. No other leader or prophet in the history of world religions ever made such a claim.

Third, *Jesus will take us to heaven personally* (John 14:3). Other religious leaders taught about the way to heaven; Jesus alone claims to take us there.

Fourth, *Jesus is the only way to the Father* (John 14:6). His Greek was emphatic: "I am the way and the truth and the life." Later, he was even more emphatic: "All authority in heaven and on earth has been given to me" (Matthew 28:18). No one in all of human history ever made this claim. Peter would later make the same announcement about Jesus (Acts 4:12).

Muhammad claimed to have recorded the revelation of Allah and the way to heaven, but he never claimed to be that way. The Buddha claimed to teach the way to enlightenment, but he was not that way. Hindu masters claim to teach the way to oneness with Brahman (reality), but none claims to be that way. Jewish rabbis claim to teach the Torah, the law of God and the way to eternal life with him, but none claims to have inspired that law or be that way to God.

Only Jesus made such a staggering claim for himself.

We may agree or disagree with him, but we need to know what he believed about himself. He never claimed to be a religious teacher or leader, or one way to God among many. He claimed to be the only way to eternity in heaven.

Of course, we would expect the Old Testament to claim that God is the only God and the New Testament to claim that Jesus is the only way to the Father. Are there objective ways to defend these claims?

What do other religions offer?

It is commonplace today to claim that the world's religions are different roads up the same mountain, different faiths in the same God. Such a claim is astonishing to those who actually follow the various faith traditions. They know that if one is right, the others are, by definition and by necessity, wrong.

Let's start with Islam.

Muslims consider the Qur'an to be the revelation of Allah (the Arabic name for "God") to humankind, given in the Arabic language. Muslims recognize five primary ways of serving Allah and gaining eternity with him (the "five pillars of Islam"):

- State with full conviction the central claim of Islam: "I bear witness that there is no God but God, and that Muhammad is his prophet."
- Pray five times each day while facing the holy city of Mecca.
- Give alms (2.5 percent of one's income and net worth) to the poor.
- Fast, especially during the holy month of Ramadan.
- Make a pilgrimage to Mecca at least once. If you are unable, provide for another to go in your place.

A sixth "pillar" is recognized by some Muslims: death during a declared holy war (a "jihad"). Muslims believe that we will live individually and consciously for all eternity, either in heaven or in hell.

Hinduism, the oldest religion in the world, [116] centers on a similar kind of works righteousness. Its famous doctrine of "karma" is illustrated by this statement in one of their sacred writings: "According as one acts, according as one conducts himself, so does he become. The doer of good becomes good. The doer of evil becomes evil. One becomes virtuous by virtuous action, bad by bad action." [117]

Hindus believe that reality ("Brahman") is the "One" who is the "source of all." Humans are "atman," a part of Brahman. Atmans are immortal: "Nobody can kill the atman; the verb 'to kill' means nothing but 'to separate the atman from the body.' The atman . . . is not born when the body is born and does not die when the body dies, whether in individual life or in cosmic life." [118]

Yoga is the spiritual discipline required to reach our identification with Brahman. Karma Yoga centers on selfless good works; Jnana Yoga stresses the path to oneness through contemplation and knowledge; Bhakti Yoga emphasizes emotion or devotion. Hindus believe that we will ultimately achieve *moksha* (salvation), where we are absorbed into Brahman and cease to exist individually.

Buddhists believe that all suffering is due to desire and that the renunciation of wrong desires leads to *nirvana* or enlightenment. They follow the Four Noble Truths:

1. Life is suffering.

2. The origin of suffering is wrong desire.

3. The cessation of wrong desire leads to the cessation of suffering.

4. The cessation of wrong desire comes from living by the Noble Eightfold Path: right view, thought, speech, action, livelihood, effort, mindfulness, and concentration.

Like Hindus, Buddhists believe that we will one day become part of reality and cease to exist as individuals.

Judaism is practiced today in three main traditions:

1. The "Orthodox" are the most committed to living by a literal interpretation of the Torah.

2. The "Conservative" are less literalistic than the Orthodox.

3. And the "Reform" are the most liberal (so much so that many among the Orthodox do not consider them true members of the faith).

However, each of these traditions focuses in its own way on obedience to the law as the means of pleasing God and receiving his mercy in eternity.

As you can see, these are very different views of eternity and salvation.

If Hindus and Buddhists are right about eternity, Muslims, Jews, and Christians must be wrong. If we achieve heaven through the five pillars of Islam, all other religions are wrong about salvation. Only Christianity offers eternal life by God's grace through faith, apart from human works (cf. Ephesians 2:8–9).

These are not different roads up the same mountain, but very different mountains.

Who is right?

There are several ways in which Christian theologians defend the superiority of their faith.

One is to consider the miraculous origin of the Christian movement. Christianity clearly stands on the factual, historical miracle of the resurrection. However, Muslims consider the inspiration and reception of the Qur'an to be miraculous; Hindus and Buddhists point to the supernatural nature of *moksha* or *nirvana*; and Jews remind us of their miraculous Exodus and the revelation of God in his word.

We doubt that followers of other faiths will concede that our faith alone can claim supernatural origin. Christians counter that the evidence for the resurrection is remarkably persuasive, but defenders of other faiths will claim the same for their founding events.

A second approach is to examine the evidence for each world religion. What proof can Muslims offer that the Qur'an was truly given by God to the illiterate Muhammad? What evidence can Buddhists offer for the enlightenment of their founder? How do Hindus really know that reincarnation is true and that *moksha* is possible?

By contrast, we have examined remarkable evidence for the trustworthiness and authority of the Bible and for the resurrection and divinity of Jesus.

However, as I (Jim) have spoken across the years with numerous followers of other faiths, I have not found this argument to be compelling for them. Every Muslim I have ever met was convinced that the Qur'an is the trustworthy revelation of God. And Hindus and Buddhists seldom seek empirical evidence for a personal, supernatural experience. (Christians have a similar problem in proving their salvation experience.)

A third response is to point to the millions of lives changed by the gospel in the decades following the birth of the church. It is an astounding fact that so many people quickly accepted the apostles' message about a crucified carpenter and that their movement would in time topple the mightiest empire the world had ever seen.

At the same time, other religions have their legions of followers as well. Islam is growing quickly all around the world. Millions of Buddhists and Hindus claim that their respective religions have transformed their lives. Jews have held to their religious convictions despite millennia of horrific persecution. If we claim that Jesus changed our lives, but you claim that the Qur'an did the same for you, we are at an impasse.

The bottom line

The fact is, we're not sure Christians can *prove* to non-Christians that our faith is right and all others are wrong. We can remove roadblocks to Christian faith that would be created if the Bible were untrustworthy or Jesus were no different from any other religious leader. By communicating the facts regarding biblical authority and Jesus' divinity, we can show the reasonable and evidential nature of our faith.

In addition, we can point to the unique nature of the Christian movement. Unlike other religions, Christianity was founded by One who claimed to be divine. Unlike other religious founders, Jesus rose from the dead. Unlike other religious movements, early Christians came to Christ despite horrendous opposition (and still continue to grow most quickly where they are persecuted most fiercely). Unlike other religious teachings, Christianity offers the absolute assurance of salvation by God's grace, received by our faith.

We admit that these facts are not so logically conclusive that they prove the truth of Christianity and the falsehood of all other faiths. Like all empirical and rational evidence, they can encourage our personal commitment, but they cannot compel it. As we have seen repeatedly, faith in Christ is like all other personal relationships: it requires a commitment transcending the evidence.

How does the Bible tell us to demonstrate the truthfulness of Christianity? Not so much by our logic as by our love. We are called to love our Lord and our neighbor (Matthew 22:34–40). We are promised that all will know that we follow Jesus when they see his love in ours (John 13:35).

Once we testify to the truth we believe and demonstrate God's love in our lives, we can trust the salvation of others to the Holy Spirit.

Human words cannot change human hearts. Only the Spirit can convict us of our sins and need for salvation. Only he can make Jesus real to those who want him. Like witnesses in a courtroom, we are responsible for telling what we have experienced. The verdict is not up to us.

I cannot convince you that Jesus is Lord, but the Holy Spirit can.

It doesn't bother us that only one key will start our cars, so long as that key works. Only Christianity works where we need God's help the most. Our basic problem with God is called "sin." We have all made mistakes and committed sins in our lives. These failures have separated us from a pure and holy God.

The only way to heaven that works is the way that deals with these sins. And only Christianity does that. No other religion offers forgiveness for sins, grace for sinners, and the security of salvation.

Only Jesus saves.

Conclusion (by Dr. Jim Denison)

When I wonder if the Christian faith can stand up to any challenge and change any life, I think about a twelve-year-old boy I met during my summer missions experience in 1979. Before I flew into Malaysia to begin my work there, I was given a week of training with career missionaries in Singapore.

One evening, as I was talking with two of these missionaries, a young boy happened to walk by. A missionary called him over and introduced him to me. He shyly shook my hand and ran off to play with his friends. Then the missionary told me his story.

This boy had come to faith in Christ during a Bible study the church conducted in his nearby apartment building. He very quickly became passionate about his Lord. He never missed a worship service on Sunday or Wednesday. He read his Bible and prayed fervently. He became a great witness to others in his community.

Soon, the missionaries began to notice bruises and welts on the young boy's body. One day they took his arm, examined the marks there, and asked him what was wrong.

The boy looked sheepishly at the ground, then answered truthfully: "My daddy is not a Christian, and when I come home from church, he beats me for worshiping Jesus."

The missionary was shocked and asked the boy why he continued coming to church.

The boy was equally surprised by the question. Looking up at the adult, he said, "But Jesus said in the Bible that we were supposed to go to church."

The missionary, mindful of many converts who had been forced from their homes, asked the boy why he stayed with his family. I'll never forget the boy's answer: "My father is not a Christian. If I leave home, he won't hear about Jesus."

So that young man went to worship, prayed and read the Scriptures, and offered God's love to the world every day. I don't know what happened to him, or if he's even alive today. But I do know that his faith was real.

On my best days, I want to follow Jesus the way that he followed Jesus. On my worst days, I still know that I should.

12

WHERE DO WE GO FROM HERE?

When we began our discussion in chapter 1, we asked the broad question, "How does God see America?" In the pages since, we've seen that, throughout Scripture, God's judgment of a nation depends on their answers to three questions:

1. Do they respect his truth?

2. Do they respect each other?

3. Do they respect him?

Whether it was with Israel or one of the pagan nations, the Lord cared deeply about the manner in which their way of life and their culture answered each of these questions. This hasn't changed.

As we have seen, there are many examples of how our culture responds to these questions in a way that God can bless. America's work to help the least of these, the biblical morality on which our country was founded (even though our culture has strayed from it in many ways), and the work we've done to help minimize the impact of racism are admirable. While there is still much work to be done, it is important to note the good that exists in our culture and our potential to be even better.

At the same time, there is also much in our nation that surely grieves the heart of God. The postmodern movement away from his objective truth and the marginalization of his word stand out. While the care demonstrated for many in need is admirable, our utter neglect and dehumanization of the unborn must be addressed. Attempts to be more inclusive of other faiths, an admirable goal in many ways, has left an increasing majority either doubting or outright rejecting the fundamental truths of the gospel.

In short, if God's judgment were based on a system of weights whereby he condemned a culture once the balance shifts in the wrong direction, we would be in danger.

Fortunately, this is not the case.

Throughout Scripture, when we see God finally bring judgment against a nation, such judgment typically comes after he has given them numerous opportunities to repent and return to him. As the perfect Father, God takes no delight in our punishment.

However, we must not mistake his patience for weakness or disinterest. A day very well may come when he decides that intervention is necessary to halt our slide away from him.

How might such judgment appear if it comes? How close are we to this point?

God's judgment in Scripture

While there is not an exact biblical criterion for when and how God will judge a nation, most of the Old Testament examples demonstrate that it falls only after a warning has been given. In Scripture, such warnings were given primarily through the prophets. However, circumstances have changed since that point in our collective history.

Prior to Jesus' incarnation, the prophets could best be described as men and women who were given a direct word from God for a certain group of people. Because Israel chose not to deal with God directly but instead chose to have him speak to intermediaries, who would then pass the message on to God, such a system was required.

Today, God speaks directly to his people through the Holy Spirit's presence in our lives. This doesn't mean that he will give every Christian a message for our nation, but it does mean that it is our responsibility to speak for him to the culture around us. If America is in need of a word from God, and we think the weight of evidence is clear that we are, such a word will come through the collective and individual voices of his people.

We have every resource we need to speak truth into our culture and help people understand where change needs to happen. This doesn't mean our nation will accept this word, but, if we haven't preached it, both through our words and especially through the way we live, then the fault lies first with us (Romans 10:14).

Even after the prophets spoke, however, God was typically patient to give a people time to respond. For the most part, a nation faced judgment only when their sins became so firmly institutionalized that they no longer considered them to be sinful. Again, this doesn't mean that every individual engages in or accepts such sin, but enough do that divine intervention is deemed necessary by God.

God's judgment of America

Because America is a democratic republic, all of us have at least some say in our governance and laws. When these laws start to formally sanction sins God condemns, we are moving in a dangerous direction.

Over the last fifty years, we have seen abortion and same-sex marriage legalized, more frequent attacks on those who stand for biblical morality, and a general acceptance of pluralism and sexual sin of both a heterosexual and homosexual nature. We think it is fair to say that, as a nation, we have largely accepted many things that God does not.

At the same time, we have also passed laws that protect and empower members of all races, that take greater care of the poor and needy, and that mandate a level of religious toleration for God's truth and his people that far exceeds what is available around much of the world. For all the areas of concern, we are not a nation devoid of aspects God can bless.

So, where is America with regard to God's judgment? To determine the answer, we need to understand the ways God often corrected the nations in Scripture.

In most of the instances where the Bible records God judging a nation, whether it was Israel or a pagan people, such punishment did not require him to take an active role. Rather, he simply stepped back to allow the natural progression of events to take place.

For example, when the ten northern tribes of Israel fell to Assyria in 722 BC, they became another nation on a long list of cultures the Assyrians conquered during that era. The same was true when Judah fell to Babylon little more than a century later.

In neither instance were God's people more outmatched than when they took the promised land under Joshua or conquered the Philistines under David. The only difference, according to God's word, is that when Israel was defeated by other nations, they did not have the Lord's blessing and protection. When they won, they did.

We doubt that America is moving toward military combat with a nation that truly poses the same kind of threat to us that the pagan peoples named above did to Israel. This does not mean, however, that our country is safe.

Whatever one believes regarding Russia's influence on the 2016 presidential election, it's clear that, at the very least, they attempted to sow seeds of chaos and division through their propaganda and manipulation of social media. China has been credibly accused of perpetrating cyber attacks against our nation and its people on multiple occasions in recent years, and there is little reason to suspect that they will stop. Terrorism poses a constant threat, even if successful attacks are far less frequent here than in a number of other countries.

When people did not repent as a result of God's passive judgment, there were times when his judgment became more active. The plagues he brought against Egypt (Exodus 7–12) are an obvious example.

Conclusion

Our point is simple: America stands in great need of God's blessing and protection. While we do not believe our nation is on the verge of collapse or that a truly existential threat is preparing to invade our land, our country faces very real dangers. Some come from outside us, but most are rising within our culture.

As a result, it's necessary to ask if we are a nation at risk of divine judgment. And it is necessary to do all we can to make a difference before it's too late.

God deals with us as gently as he can or as harshly as he must, but the testimony of Scripture is clear that he will not let sin go unpunished forever. Whether it is through natural or supernatural circumstances, God longs to help us turn back to himself. The severity of such judgment is often directly linked to the stubbornness of those being judged.

This book was written to equip God's people to identify beliefs and behaviors God cannot bless and then to encourage us to use our influence to make a transformative impact on our nation. When Jesus called his followers "the salt of the earth" and "the light of the world" (Matthew 5:13, 14), he used definite articles to indicate that we are the only salt and light in our decaying, darkening world.

It is a great responsibility and privilege to use our spiritual gifts and cultural influence to make an eternal difference for our Lord.

Imagine for a moment what our nation could be if every Christian not only agreed with this fact but lived it out as well. We've seen such a spiritual movement in our nation's past. If we are to see one again, it must begin with God's people (2 Chronicles 7:13–14).

Could it begin with you?

About the Authors

Dr. Jim Denison is the Chief Executive Officer of Denison Forum.

Through *The Daily Article*, his free email newsletter and podcast that globally reach 160,000+ subscribers, Dr. Denison guides readers to discern today's news — biblically.

He has written multiple books and has taught on the philosophy of religion and apologetics. Before launching Denison Forum in 2009, he pastored churches in Texas and Georgia. He holds a PhD and an MDiv from Southwestern Baptist Theological Seminary and a DD from Dallas Baptist University.

Jim and his wife, Janet, live in Dallas, Texas. They have two sons and four grandchildren.

Ryan Denison is the Senior Fellow for Theology at Denison Forum.

He consults on *The Daily Article* and provides writing and research for many of the ministry's productions.

He is in the final stages of earning his PhD in church history at BH Carroll Theological Institute after having earned his MDiv at Truett Seminary. Ryan has also taught at BH Carroll and Dallas Baptist University.

He and his wife, Candice, live in East Texas and have two children.

Appendix:
Help for those
considering suicide

People consider suicide when the pain they feel exceeds their ability to cope with it. They want to end their suffering and think that ending their lives will bring relief.

If you or someone you know is having thoughts of suicide, please get help immediately. Ask your pastor to recommend a Christian counselor in your area. You can call the National Suicide Prevention Lifeline at 1-800-273-8255 (TALK) or go to the National Suicide Prevention Lifeline's website at suicidepreventionlifeline.org. Take every threat of suicide seriously.

In the meanwhile, it is important to know that it is possible to get through this. Feeling suicidal does not require that we act on our feeling. The best thing to do immediately is to create some space. If we decide not to act on our feelings for even a few minutes or a day, we can find the strength to seek help. By seeking help, we can deal with the pain and find the hope we need.

Warning signs

The Centers for Disease Control lists these twelve "suicide warning signs":

- Feeling like a burden
- Being isolated

- Increased anxiety
- Feeling trapped or in unbearable pain
- Increased substance use
- Looking for a way to access lethal means
- Increased anger or rage
- Extreme mood swings
- Expressing hopelessness
- Sleeping too little or too much
- Talking or posting about wanting to die
- Making plans for suicide[119]

This is an issue parents need to discuss with their children. I urge you to read Janet Denison's blog, "The Kate Spade Conversation."[120] She discusses the major rise in depression among teenagers and links to an important article by the Society to Prevent Teenage Suicide.

And she notes that "too often, Christians feel that depression should simply be handled 'spiritually' instead of 'medically.' Depression is an illness, and an illness needs both types of help. If you have reason to believe your child is clinically depressed, you and your child need the help of a physician, as well as the Great Physician."

Protective factors

The following indicators help buffer people from the risks associated with suicide:

- Effective clinical care for mental, physical, and substance abuse disorders
- Easy access to clinical interventions and support for those seeking help
- Family and community support
- Support from ongoing medical and mental health care relationships

- Skills in problem-solving, conflict resolution, and nonviolent ways of handling disputes
- Cultural and religious beliefs that discourage suicide and encourage self-preservation instincts [121]

Help those you care about to experience these positive influences and you'll do much to prevent the tragedy of suicide.

ENDNOTES

Chapter One:
A Brief History of Truth: How The Truth Became "My Truth"

[1] The prophets often included portents of judgment against the pagan nations alongside their warnings to Israel and Judah, and often for similar sins. By the time of the exile, there appears to have been little that separated the actions and general approach to God by the Hebrews from that of the nations around them.

[2] Thomas S. Kidd, *God of Liberty* (New York: Basic Books, 2010), 211.

[3] What follows are merely a few of the many examples that demonstrate the impact of the Great Awakenings on American culture.

[4] Philip Yancey, "God on the Move," (https://philipyancey.com/god-on-the-move, accessed 19 September 2016).

[5] While this passage in Genesis speaks to Israel's purpose of being a blessing to "all peoples on earth," Scripture repeatedly notes that God's truth as passed down through his word is a blessing to those who experience it and the key to engaging in the kind of abundant life he longs to give. Consequently, it is logical to conclude that a fundamental element of Israel's purpose as a blessing to other nations could only be fulfilled in helping them know and appreciate God's word.

[6] We will take a closer look at these types of sins in subsequent sections.

[7] Nineveh was the capital of Assyria when Jonah went there during the reign of the wicked Israelite king Jeroboam II (786–746 BC). The Assyrians would capture Israel and make Judah a vassal state in 722 BC.

[8] Aristotle also played a crucial role in laying the final pieces upon which much of Western civilization's foundation was built, but the majority of his contributions lie in areas that are not immediately pertinent to our conversation about the nature of truth.

[9] Skipping over such influential thinkers as Augustine, Anselm, and St. Thomas, not to mention most of the Protestant Reformation era thinkers like Erasmus, Luther, and Calvin is difficult but necessary for our present efforts. Their contributions, while enormously significant, were less relevant to the basic understanding of truth.

Chapter Two:
The Impotence of Scripture: Why "God's Word Says" No Longer Matters to Our Culture

[10] Christopher Hitchens, *god is not Great: How Religion Poisons Everything* (New York: Twelve, 2007) 282.

[11] Ibid., 102, 120.

[12] Norman Geisler and Ron Brooks, *When Skeptics Ask: A Handbook on Christian Evidences* (Wheaton, Illinois: Victor Books, 1990) 91.

[13] This discussion follows the treatment by Josh McDowell, *The New Evidence that Demands a Verdict* (Nashville: Thomas Nelson, 1999) 167–94. McDowell's discussion is helpful in that it depends heavily upon Jewish interpretation of the Old Testament sources cited.

Chapter Three:
The Tolerance of Unbiblical Sexuality: How the LGBTQ Agenda Violates God's Will

[14] Sarah Pulliam Bailey, "Poll shows a dramatic generational divide in white evangelical attitudes on gay marriage," The Washington Post, June 27, 2017 (https://www.washingtonpost.com/news/acts-of-faith/wp/2017/06/27/there-is-now-a-dramatic-generational-divide-over-white-evangelical-attitudes-on-gay-marriage/, accessed 7 March 2019).

[15] Walter Wink, "Homosexuality and the Bible" (http://media1.razorplanet.com/share/510599-9786/resources/1208823_HomosexualityandtheBibleWalterWink.pdf, accessed 7 March 2019).

[16] Peter Gomes, *The Good Book: Reading the Bible with Mind and Heart* (New York: Avon Books, 1992) 150–2, 164.

[17] Cited by Ronald M. Springett, "What Does the Old Testament Say About Homosexuality?" *The Crisis of Homosexuality*, ed. J. Isamu Yamamoto (Wheaton, Illinois: Victor Books, 1990) 135.

[18] Everett Fox, ed., *The Five Books of Moses*, The Schocken Bible: Volume I (New York: Schocken Books, 1995) 80.

[19] Wink.

[20] See Gordon D. Fee and Douglas Stuart, *How to Read the Bible for All Its Worth: A Guide to Understanding the Bible*, 2nd. ed. (Grand Rapids, Michigan: Zondervan, 1993) 153–4.

[21] "Answers to Your Questions For a Better Understanding of Sexual Orientation & Homosexuality," *American Psychological Association*, 2008 (http://www.apa.org/topics/sexuality/sorientation.pdf, accessed 7 March 2019).

22 "Gays more prone to depression," health24 (http://www.health24.com/Medical/Depression/News/Gays-more-prone-to-depression-20120721, accessed 7 March 2019).

23 J. Bradford, et. al., "National Lesbian Health Care Survey: Implications for mental health care," *National Center for Biotechnology Information*, April 1994 (http://www.ncbi.nlm.nih.gov/pubmed/8201059, accessed 7 March 2019).

24 Matt Slick, "Homosexual activity doesn't harm anyone," *Christian Apologetics & Research Ministry* (http://carm.org/homosexual-gay-sex-harms-no-one, accessed 7 March 2019).

25 "HIV Among Black/African American Gay, Bisexual, and Other Men Who Have Sex With Men," *Centers for Disease Control and Prevention* (http://www.cdc.gov/hiv/risk/racialethnic/bmsm/facts/index.html, accessed 7 March 2019).

26 John R. Diggs, Jr., M.D., "The Health Risks of Gay Sex," *Catholic Education Resource Center* (http://www.catholiceducation.org/en/marriage-and-family/sexuality/the-health-risks-of-gay-sex.html, accessed 7 March 2019).

Chapter Four:
The Subjectivity of Gender Identity: How Transgenderism Confuses the Culture

27 "Answers to Your Questions About Transgender People, Gender Identity and Gender Expression," *American Psychological Association* (http://www.apa.org/topics/lgbt/transgender.aspx, accessed 11 March 2019).

28 "Gender dysphoria," *Psychology Today* (https://www.psychologytoday.com/conditions/gender-dysphoria, accessed 11 March 2019).

29 Jessica Hamzelou, "Transsexual differences caught on brain scan," *New Scientist*, January 26, 2011 (https://www.newscientist.com/article/dn20032-transsexual-differences-caught-on-brain-scan#.UhKQTBYx-5c, accessed 11 March 2019).

30 Francine Russo, "Is There Something Unique about the Transgender Brain?" *Scientific American*, January 1, 2016 (http://www.scientificamerican.com/article/is-there-something-unique-about-the-transgender-brain/, accessed 11 March 2019).

31 R. S. Soleman, et. al., "Sex differences in verbal fluency during adolescence: a functional magnetic resonance imaging study in gender dysphoric and control boys and girls," *Journal of Sexual Medicine*, August 10, 2013 (http://www.ncbi.nlm.nih.gov/pubmed/23433223, accessed 11 March 2019).

32 L. Hare, et. al., "Androgen receptor repeat length polymorphism associated with male-to-female transsexualism," *Biological Psychiatry*, January 1, 2009 (http://www.ncbi.nlm.nih.gov/pmc/articles/PMC3402034/, accessed 11 March 2019).

33 Eileen Luders, et. al., "Regional gray matter variation in male-to-female transsexualism," *Neuroimage*, July 15, 2009 (http://www.ncbi.nlm.nih.gov/pmc/articles/PMC2754583/, accessed 11 March 2019).

[34] A. Garcia-Falgueras, et. al., "Galanin neurons in the intermediate nucleus (InM) of the human hypothalamus in relation to sex, age, and gender identity," *Journal of Comparative Neurology*, October 15, 2011 (http://www.ncbi.nlm.nih.gov/pubmed/21618223, accessed 11 March 2019).

[35] Milton Diamond, "Transsexuality Among Twins: Identity Concordance, Transition, Rearing, and Orientation," *International Journal of Transgenderism*, May 2013 (http://www.hawaii.edu/PCSS/biblio/articles/2010to2014/2013-transsexuality.html, accessed 11 March 2019).

[36] Benedetta Leuner, Erica R. Glasper, and Elizabeth Gould, "Parenting and plasticity," *National Institutes of Health, U.S. National Library of Medicine*, April 13, 2011 (http://www.ncbi.nlm.nih.gov/pmc/articles/PMC3076301/, accessed 11 March 20190).

[37] For example, perhaps a man feels drawn to tasks that rely more on compassion than strength or aggression.

[38] Zach Ford, "STUDY: Transgender People Experience Discrimination Trying to Use Bathrooms," *The Williams Institute*, June 26, 2013 (http://williamsinstitute.law.ucla.edu/press/study-transgender-people-experience-discrimination-trying-to-use-bathrooms/, accessed 11 March 2019).

[39] Julie Hirschfeld Davis, "Obama Defends Transgender Directive for School Bathrooms," *The New York Times*, May 16, 2016 (http://www.nytimes.com/2016/05/17/us/politics/obama-defends-transgender-directive-for-school-bathrooms.html?_r=0, accessed 11 March 2019).

Section Two: How do Americans Relate to Each Other?
Introduction

[40] John notes: "To all who did receive him, who believed in his name, he gave the right to become children of God" (John 1:12). Paul echoed these sentiments when describing our adoption by God (Romans 8:16–17, Ephesians 1:5). As a result, only those who have trusted in Christ are commonly referred to as the children of God. As we will soon see, however, that distinction refers more to the reality of our relationship to God than the degree to which he loves everyone.

Chapter Five
Killing the Unborn: Why Abortion Is a Choice None Should Make

[41] "Roe v. Wade," *FindLaw for Legal Professionals* (https://caselaw.findlaw.com/us-supreme-court/410/113.html, accessed 11 March 2019).

[42] Ibid.

[43] We are starting to see this argument extended to infanticide and euthanasia more frequently, further demonstrating the connection.

44 "Pregnancy week by week," *Mayo Clinic* (https://www.mayoclinic.org/healthy-lifestyle/pregnancy-week-by-week/in-depth/prenatal-care/art-20045302, accessed 13 March 2019).

45 Kristi Burton Brown, "What really happens during a suction D&C abortion?" *Live Action*, March 4, 2016 (https://www.liveaction.org/news/what-really-happens-during-a-dc-abortion/, accessed 13 March 2019).

46 "The Second Trimester: Your Baby's Growth and Development in Middle Pregnancy," *WebMD* (https://www.webmd.com/baby/4to6-months, accessed 13 March 2019).

47 Emma Green, "Science Is Giving the Pro-Life Movement a Boost," *The Atlantic*, January 18, 2018 (https://www.theatlantic.com/politics/archive/2018/01/pro-life-pro-science/549308/, accessed 13 March 2019).

48 "List of methods of capital punishment," Wikipedia (https://en.wikipedia.org/wiki/List_of_methods_of_capital_punishment, accessed 13 March 2019).

49 "Animal slaughter," Wikipedia (https://en.wikipedia.org/wiki/Animal_slaughter, accessed 13 March 2019).

50 For a larger discussion, see Jim Denison, *7 Critical Issues: The State of Our Nation* (2016) 51–60.

51 Felicity Barringer, "THE 1992 CAMPAIGN: Campaign Issues; Clinton and Gore Shifted on Abortion," *The New York Times*, July 20, 1992 (https://www.nytimes.com/1992/07/20/us/the-1992-campaign-campaign-issues-clinton-and-gore-shifted-on-abortion.html, accessed 12 March 2019).

Chapter Six
Caring Little for the Least: How the Poor, the Sick, the Foreign, and the Jailed Reveal America's True Face

52 There is some debate that the "least of these" in this passage references the needy in general rather than specifically Christians in need. I believe the former to be the most accurate reading of the passage, but, even if that is not the case, Scripture provides abundant examples of God's concern for those in need. Consequently, even if someone disagrees with this chapter's understanding of the "least of these" as it relates to Matthew 25, the principles still hold.

53 "The Population of Poverty USA," *PovertyUSA* (https://povertyusa.org/facts, accessed 5 March 2019).

54 "U.S. Poverty Statistics," Federal Safety Net (http://federalsafetynet.com/us-poverty-statistics.html, accessed 5 March 2019).

55 "Health Insurance Coverage in the United States: 2017," *The United States Census Bureau* (https://www.census.gov/library/publications/2018/demo/p60-264.html, accessed 13 March 2019).

[56] Gustavo López, Kristen Bialik, and Jynnah Radford, "Key findings about U.S. immigrants," *Pew Research Center*, November 30, 2018 (http://www.pewresearch.org/fact-tank/2018/11/30/key-findings-about-u-s-immigrants/, accessed 13 March 2019). All of the immigration statistics that follow come from this study as well.

[57] Ibid.

[58] Danielle Kaeble and Mary Cowhig, "Correctional Populations in the United States, 2016," U.S. Department of Justice, April 2018 (https://www.bjs.gov/content/pub/pdf/cpus16.pdf, accessed 15 March 2019).

[59] C. S. Lewis, *Mere Christianity* (New York: HarperCollins, 2001 [1952]) 134.

Chapter Seven
Doubting that Racism Exists: Why the Fight Against Racism Has Always Been Biblical

[60] Art Swift, "Americans' Worries About Race Relations at Record High," *Gallup*, March 15, 2017 (https://news.gallup.com/poll/206057/americans-worry-race-relations-record-high.aspx, accessed 13 March 2019).

[61] "2016 Hate Crime Statistics Released," *FBI News*, November 13, 2017 (https://www.fbi.gov/news/stories/2016-hate-crime-statistics, accessed 13 March 2019).

[62] Richard Florida, "Where Hate Groups Are Concentrated in the U.S.," *Citylab*, March 15, 2018 (https://www.citylab.com/equity/2018/03/where-hate-groups-are-concentrated-in-the-us/555689/, accessed 13 March 2019).

[63] "Racism," *Oxford English Dictionary* (https://en.oxforddictionaries.com/definition/racism, accessed 13 March 2019).

[64] Sean P. Harvey, "Ideas of Race in Early America," *American History: Oxford Research Encyclopedias*, April 2016 (http://americanhistory.oxfordre.com/view/10.1093/acrefore/9780199329175.001.0001/acrefore-9780199329175-e-262, accessed 13 March 2019).

[65] Ibid; italics in the original.

[66] "The Origins and Growth of Slavery in America," *American History Rules* (http://americanhistoryrules.com/divisionandreunion/the-origins-of-slavery-in-america/, accessed 13 March 2019).

[67] "Slavery, the Constitution, and a Lasting Legacy," *The Robert H. Smith Center for the Constitution at James Madison's Montpelier* (https://www.montpelier.org/learn/slavery-constitution-lasting-legacy, accessed 13 March 2019).

[68] "Racism," *The National Museum of American History* (http://americanhistory.si.edu/righting-wrong-japanese-americans-and-world-war-ii/racism, accessed 13 March 2019).

[69] Jeff Nesbit, "Institutional Racism Is Our Way of Life," U.S. News & World Report, May 6, 2015 (https://www.usnews.com/news/blogs/at-the-edge/2015/05/06/institutional-racism-is-our-way-of-life, accessed 13 March 2019).

[70] Ruth Moon, "Does the Gospel Mandate Racial Reconciliation? White Pastors Agree More Than Black Pastors," *Christianity Today*, December 16, 2014 (https://www.christianitytoday.com/news/2014/december/does-gospel-mandate-racial-reconciliation-lifeway-kainos.html, accessed 13 March 2019).

[71] "Black Lives Matter and Racial Tension in America," *Barna*, May 5, 2016 (https://www.barna.com/research/black-lives-matter-and-racial-tension-in-america/#.V45Hf5MrKb8, accessed 13 March 2019).

[72] Bob Smietana, "Sunday Morning Segregation: Most Worshipers Feel Their Church Has Enough Diversity," *Christianity Today*, January 15, 2015 (https://www.christianitytoday.com/news/2015/january/sunday-morning-segregation-most-worshipers-church-diversity.html, accessed 13 March 2019).

[73] Adelle M. Banks, "Some Protestant pastors preach on race but most leave it to others," *Religion News Service*, March 30, 2017 (https://religionnews.com/2017/03/30/some-protestant-pastors-preach-on-race-but-most-leave-it-to-others/, accessed 13 March 2019).

[74] *The Scofield Reference Bible*, ed. C. I. Scofield (New York: Oxford University Press, 1909) 16.

[75] Tony Evans, "Are Black People Cursed? The Curse of Ham," Eternal Perspective Ministries, January 18, 2010 (https://www.epm.org/resources/2010/Jan/18/are-black-people-cursed-curse-ham/, accessed 13 March 2019).

[76] For these and other examples, see John P. Newport and William Cannon, *Why Christians Fight Over the Bible* (Nashville: Thomas Nelson, 1974) 163-4.

[77] Andrew Arenge, Stephanie Perry and Dartunorro Clark, "Poll: 64 percent of Americans say racism remains a major problem," *NBC News*, May 29, 2018 (https://www.nbcnews.com/politics/politics-news/poll-64-percent-americans-say-racism-remains-major-problem-n877536, accessed 13 March 2019).

[78] C. S. Lewis, *Mere Christianity* (New York: HarperCollins, 2001 [1952]) 128.

[79] Sarah Kaplan and William Wan, "Why are people still racist? What science says about America's race problem," *The Washington Post*, August 14, 2017 (https://www.washingtonpost.com/news/speaking-of-science/wp/2017/08/14/why-are-people-still-racist-what-science-says-about-americas-race-problem/, accessed 13 March 2019).

[80] Ibid.

[81] Julissa Higgins, "Read George W. Bush's Speech at the Dallas Shooting Memorial Service," *Time*, July 12, 2016 (http://time.com/4403510/george-w-bush-speech-dallas-shooting-memorial-service/, accessed 13 March 2019).

[82] Tony Evans, "America's current violence can be traced to Christians' failures," *The Washington Post*, July 9, 2016 (https://www.washingtonpost.com/news/acts-of-faith/wp/2016/07/09/americas-current-violence-can-be-traced-to-christians-failures/, accessed 13 March 2019).

[83] Justin Martyr, *The First Apology* 14 (http://www.newadvent.org/fathers/0126.htm, accessed 13 March 2019).

84 Clement of Alexandria, Miscellanies 7.77 (https://books.google.com books?id=ZMX0yk Rov6YC&pg=PA135&lpg=PA135&dq=He+impoverishes+himself+out+of+love,+ clement+of+alexandria&source=bl&ots=POzz_gQq1w&sig=1R_YgEmVX-426oZmwqwy h1gp_QI&hl=en&sa=X&ved=0ahUKEwjg1Yr4mqfcAhXM7IMKHV_qADkQ6AEIODAD #v=onepage&q=He%20impoverishes%20himself%20out%20of%20love%2C%20 clement%20of%20alexandria&f=false, accessed 13 March 2019).

85 "The Octavius of Minucius Felix," *Ante-Nicene Fathers* 4.31 (https://st-takla.org/ books/en/ecf/004/0040034.html, accessed 13 March 2019).

86 Quoted in "What Were Early Christians Like?" *Christianity.com* (https://www. christianity.com/church/church-history/timeline/1-300/what-were-early-christians-like-11629560.html, accessed 13 March 2019).

Chapter Eight
Killing Ourselves: Why Suicide Isn't Unpardonable

87 Dennis Thompson, "More Americans suffering from stress, anxiety and depression, study finds," *CBS News*, April 17, 2017 (https://www.cbsnews.com/ news/stress-anxiety-depression-mental-illness-increases-study-finds/, accessed 13 March 2019).

88 "Understand the Facts," *Anxiety and Depression Association of America* (https:// adaa.org/understanding-anxiety, accessed 13 March 2019).

89 Nick Zagorski, "Many Prescription Opioids Go to Adults With Depression, Anxiety," *Psychiatric News*, August 17, 2017 (https://psychnews.psychiatryonline. org/doi/full/10.1176/appi.pn.2017.8a13, accessed 13 March 2019).

90 "Substance Use Disorders," *Anxiety and Depression Association of America* (https://adaa.org/understanding-anxiety/related-illnesses/substance-abuse, accessed 13 March 2019).

91 "Anxiety and physical illness," *Harvard Health Publishing*, May 9, 2018 (https:// www.health.harvard.edu/staying-healthy/anxiety_and_physical_illness, accessed 13 March 2019).

92 Claire Mokrysz, "Patients with anxiety disorders are more likely to have suicidal thoughts and actions, says recent review," *The Mental Elf* (https://www. nationalelfservice.net/mental-health/anxiety/patients-with-anxiety-disorders-are-more-likely-to-have-suicidal-thoughts-and-actions-says-recent-review/, accessed 13 March 2019).

93 Sources for this study include: *Catechism of the Catholic Church*, second edition English translation; the National Center for Injury Prevention and Control (www. ced.gov/ncipc); T. Clemons, "Suicide," *International Standard Bible Encyclopedia*, ed. Geoffrey W. Bromiley (Grand Rapids: Eerdmans, 1988) 4:652–3; A. J.

Droge, "Suicide," *The Anchor Bible Dictionary*, ed. David Noel Freedman (New York: Doubleday, 1992) 6:225–31; Milton A. Gonsalves, *Fagothey's Right and Reason: Ethics in Theory and Practice*, 9th ed. (Columbus: Merrill Publishing Company, 1989) 246–8; the Suicide Awareness Voices of Education (www.save. org); and the American Association of Suicidology (www.suicidology.org).

94 "Suicide by Age," *Suicide Prevention Resource Center* (http://www.sprc.org/scope/age, accessed 13 March 2019).

95 Benedict Carey, "Defying Prevention Efforts, Suicide Rates Are Climbing Across the Nation," *The New York Times*, June 7, 2018 (https://www.nytimes.com/2018/06/07/health/suicide-rates-kate-spade.html, accessed 13 March 2019).

96 Rae Ellen Bichell, "Suicide Rates Climb In U.S., Especially Among Adolescent Girls," *NPR*, April 22, 2016 (https://www.npr.org/sections/health-shots/2016/04/22/474888854/suicide-rates-climb-in-u-s-especially-among-adolescent-girls, accessed 13 March 2019).

97 Philip Perry, "This may be responsible for the high suicide rate among white, American men," *Big Think*, July 2, 2017 (https://bigthink.com/philip-perry/this-may-be-responsible-for-the-high-suicide-rate-among-white-american-men, accessed 13 March 2019).

98 "Suicide rising across the US," *Centers for Disease Control and Prevention* (https://www.cdc.gov/vitalsigns/suicide/, accessed 13 March 2019).

99 Carey.

100 C. S. Lewis, *The Problem of Pain* (New York: Macmillan, 1977 [1940]) 156.

101 C. S. Lewis, "The Weight of Glory," in *The Weight of Glory and Other Addresses* (New York: HarperCollins, 2001 [1949]) 46.

Section 3: How do Americans Relate to God?
Introduction

102 C. S. Lewis, "Is Theology Poetry," in *The Weight of Glory and Other Addresses* (New York: HarperCollins, 2001 [1949]) 92.

Chapter Nine
Is God Real?

103 J. L. Mackie, *The Miracle of Theism: Arguments for and against the Existence of God* (Oxford: Clarendon Press, 1982) 10.

104 J. P. Moreland and Kai Nielsen, *Does God Exist? The Great Debate* (Nashville, Tennessee: Thomas Nelson, 1990) 35.

[105] Sam Harris, *Letter to a Christian Nation* (New York City, New York: Knopf, 2006) 51.

[106] See, for instance, Kai Nielsen, "No! A Defense of Atheism," in *Does God Exist?* pp. 48–63.

[107] Harris 52.

Chapter Ten
Is Jesus Really God?

[108] C. S. Lewis, *Mere Christianity* (New York: HarperCollins, 2001 [1952]) 52.

[109] Gary Habermas and Antony Flew, *Did Jesus Rise From the Dead? The Resurrection Debate*, ed. Terry L. Miethe (San Francisco: Harper & Row, 1987) 23.

[110] Moreland 40.

[111] Ibid.

[112] David Hume, *An Enquiry Concerning Human Understanding* (LaSalle, Illinois: Open Court, 1966 [1907]) 128–9.

[113] Their critics' statement that they were "unschooled, ordinary men" (Acts 4:13) meant that they had not attended the rabbinic schools (the seminaries of the day), not that they were unintelligent or uneducated.

[114] The punishment Jesus endured prior to his crucifixion was enough to kill many men and left him on the brink of death before the nails or the cross ever touched his flesh.

Chapter Eleven
Is Jesus the Only Way to God?

[115] "Many Americans Say Other Faiths Can Lead to Eternal Life," *Pew Research Center*, December 18, 2008 (http://www.pewforum.org/2008/12/18/many-americans-say-other-faiths-can-lead-to-eternal-life/, accessed 14 March 2019).

[116] Most scholars agree that Judaism, as a religion, started with Abraham rather than Adam, even though humanity's relationship with God is traced back to the latter. Since Hinduism predates Abraham, it is seen as the oldest religion.

[117] From the *Brihadaranyaka Upanishad*, in *Sacred Texts of the World: A Universal Anthology*, ed. Ninian Smart and Richard D. Hecht (New York: Crossroad, 1982) 193.

[118] "Commentary to the Bhagavad-Gita," in *Sacred Texts* 203.

Appendix
Help for Those Considering Suicide

[119] "Suicide rising across the US."

[120] "Janet Denison, "The Kate Spade Conversation," *ChristianParenting*.org, June 7, 2018 (http://www.christianparenting.org/articles/kate-spade-conversation/, accessed 13 March 2019).

[121] "Suicide: Risk and Protective Factors," *Centers for Disease Control and Prevention* (https://www.cdc.gov/violenceprevention/suicide/riskprotectivefactors.html, accessed 13 March 2019).